Python Multi-paradigm Expertise:

A Detailed Guide to Object-Oriented, Functional, and Procedural Programming for Creating Neat, High-Performance Code and Constructing Adaptable Applications

Matthew D.Passmore

1

TABLE OF CONTENT

WHAT IS PROCEDURAL PROGRAMMING?

Breaking Down Programs into Functions
Understanding Control Flow

WRITING MODULAR CODE

Creating Reusable Functions
Organizing Code into Modules and Packages

.

CHAPTER 8: Advanced Procedural Programming

OPTIMIZING ALGORITHMS FOR PERFORMANCE

Efficient Sorting and Searching Techniques
Complexity Analysis and Optimization

UTILIZING MULTI-THREADING AND CONCURRENCY

Understanding Python's GIL
Implementing Concurrency with Threads and Asyncio

Choosing the Right Paradigms for Each Component

IMPLEMENTING AND TESTING YOUR APPLICATION

Writing and Testing Code in Different Paradigms
Debugging and Optimizing for Performance

PART VI: PYTHON TOOLS AND BEST PRACTICES

CHAPTER 11: Essential Tools for Python Development

INTEGRATED DEVELOPMENT ENVIRONMENTS (IDEs)

Choosing the Right IDE for Your Workflow
Maximizing Productivity with IDE Features

VERSION CONTROL AND COLLABORATION

Using Git for Source Control
Collaborating with Teams on Python Projects

CHAPTER 12: Writing Clean and Maintainable Python Code

FOLLOWING PYTHONIC CONVENTIONS

Understanding PEP 8 Standards
Writing Code That's Readable and Consistent

TESTING AND DEBUGGING TECHNIQUES

Unit Testing with PyTest
Effective Debugging Strategies

PART I: INTRODUCTION TO PYTHON PROGRAMMING

CHAPTER 1
Understanding Python as a Multi-Paradigm Language

Python is renowned for its flexibility and versatility, making it one of the most popular programming languages in the world. A key factor in this popularity is Python's ability to support multiple programming paradigms, including object-oriented, functional, and procedural programming. This multi-paradigm capability allows developers to choose the best tools and techniques for a given task, leading to cleaner, more efficient, and more adaptable code.

In this chapter, we will explore what it means for Python to be a multi-paradigm language, highlighting how it enables developers to switch seamlessly between different styles of programming. We will start by defining what programming paradigms are and why they matter. From there, we will delve into the specific paradigms that Python supports, providing examples of how Python's syntax and features align with each approach.

Additionally, this chapter will examine the practical benefits of multi-paradigm programming. We will discuss scenarios where combining paradigms can lead to more robust and maintainable codebases, as well as cases where a specific paradigm may be more advantageous. By the end of this chapter, readers will have a comprehensive understanding of how Python's multi-paradigm nature empowers them to tackle a wide range of programming challenges effectively.

This foundational knowledge will set the stage for deeper dives into each paradigm in the following parts of the book, equipping you with the skills to write elegant and powerful Python code across various programming contexts.

WHAT IS MULTI-PARADIGM PROGRAMMING?

Multi-paradigm programming is a programming approach that allows developers to utilize different programming paradigms—such as object-oriented, functional, and procedural—within the same language or application. This approach offers the flexibility to choose the most suitable paradigm for specific tasks, leading to more expressive, maintainable, and efficient code.

In the context of Python, multi-paradigm programming means that you can write code using object-oriented principles, where data and behavior are encapsulated in classes and objects. Simultaneously, you can employ functional programming techniques, leveraging first-class functions, immutability, and higher-order functions for operations like mapping, filtering, and reducing data. Additionally, Python's procedural programming capabilities allow you to organize your code into simple, linear sequences of instructions, making it easier to implement straightforward logic and control flow.

The ability to switch between these paradigms—or even combine them—within a single program is a significant strength of Python. It enables developers to apply the best tool for the job, whether they are building large-scale applications, data pipelines, or simple scripts. Understanding and mastering multi-paradigm programming in Python not only enhances your coding versatility but also helps you develop solutions that are more aligned with the problem domain, leading to clearer, more robust, and adaptable software.

This chapter will introduce the core concepts of multi-paradigm programming, discuss the benefits and challenges of this approach, and provide examples of how Python supports and integrates multiple paradigms seamlessly. By the end, you will have a solid foundation in multi-paradigm programming, ready to explore each paradigm in detail as you advance through the book.

Defining Programming Paradigms

Programming paradigms are fundamental styles or approaches to writing code, each with its own set of principles, patterns, and methodologies. They provide a framework for thinking about software design and development, guiding how problems are approached and solutions are implemented.

At their core, programming paradigms influence the structure and organization of code, dictating how data is represented, how operations are performed, and how different parts of a program interact with each other. Each paradigm offers a unique perspective on problem-solving, often rooted in different philosophies and conceptual models.

Here are the primary programming paradigms:

Procedural Programming:
Procedural programming is one of the oldest and most straightforward paradigms. It is based on the concept of procedure calls, where a program is a sequence of instructions executed in a linear, step-by-step manner. This paradigm organizes code into functions or procedures, which encapsulate specific tasks or operations. It emphasizes a clear, top-down approach to problem-solving, making it easy to follow and debug. In procedural programming, the focus is on the sequence of actions or commands to manipulate data, often leading to code that is simple and easy to understand.

Object-Oriented Programming (OOP):
Object-oriented programming is a paradigm centered around the concept of "objects," which are instances of classes. In OOP, data and the operations that manipulate that data are bundled together into objects. This paradigm promotes the use of encapsulation, inheritance, and

polymorphism to create reusable and modular code. OOP allows developers to model real-world entities more naturally, making it easier to manage complex systems and create extensible, maintainable codebases.

Functional Programming:
Functional programming is a paradigm that treats computation as the evaluation of mathematical functions and avoids changing-state and mutable data. It emphasizes the use of pure functions, where the same inputs will always produce the same outputs, without side effects. Functional programming promotes a declarative style, where the focus is on what to solve rather than how to solve it. This approach leads to code that is more predictable, easier to test, and often more concise.

Declarative Programming:

Declarative programming is a broader paradigm that encompasses functional programming but also includes other styles like logic programming and domain-specific languages. In declarative programming, you specify what the program should accomplish without explicitly detailing how to achieve it. The paradigm abstracts the control flow, allowing the language or framework to handle the underlying execution details. This approach can simplify complex tasks, especially in areas like database queries or UI design, by focusing on the desired outcomes rather than the steps to reach them.

Each of these paradigms has its strengths and is suited to different types of problems. Some languages are designed with a single paradigm in mind, while others, like Python, are multi-paradigm, meaning they support multiple paradigms within the same language. Understanding these paradigms allows developers to select the most appropriate tools and techniques for their projects, leading to more effective and efficient coding practices.

In the context of Python, mastering these paradigms enables developers to leverage the language's full potential, combining different approaches to create robust, flexible, and maintainable software solutions.

Why Python Excels in Multiple Paradigms

Python's widespread popularity and versatility stem largely from its ability to support multiple programming paradigms seamlessly. Unlike many programming languages that are designed with a specific paradigm in mind, Python was built to be flexible, allowing developers to choose the best paradigm for the task at hand. This multi-paradigm capability is one of the key reasons why Python excels in a variety of domains, from web development and data science to automation and artificial intelligence.

Here's why Python is particularly well-suited to multiple paradigms:

Simplicity and Readability:
Python's syntax is designed to be clean and easy to understand, regardless of the paradigm being used. This simplicity allows developers to write code in a procedural, object-oriented, or functional style without the language itself getting in the way. Python's focus on readability ensures that code remains accessible and maintainable, even when combining different paradigms within a single project.

Rich Standard Library:
Python's extensive standard library includes modules and tools that support various paradigms out of the box. For procedural programming, Python provides robust tools for flow control, data manipulation, and system interaction. For

object-oriented programming, Python offers built-in support for classes, inheritance, and polymorphism. In functional programming, Python includes features like first-class functions, list comprehensions, and modules like functools that support functional constructs. This diverse standard library empowers developers to adopt different paradigms as needed, without requiring additional libraries or frameworks.

First-Class Functions:
Python treats functions as first-class objects, meaning they can be passed around, stored in data structures, and manipulated like any other object. This characteristic is crucial for both functional and object-oriented programming, enabling developers to write higher-order functions, create callbacks, and implement design patterns that rely on function objects. The ability to easily mix functions with objects and data structures is a significant advantage when combining paradigms.

Dynamic Typing:
Python's dynamic typing system allows for greater flexibility when working with different paradigms. In an object-oriented context, dynamic typing enables polymorphism, where different objects can be treated as

instances of the same class. In a functional context, dynamic typing allows functions to accept and return a wide variety of data types without requiring rigid type declarations. This flexibility makes it easier to switch between paradigms and to integrate them in complex applications.

Support for Procedural, Object-Oriented, and Functional Programming:

Python natively supports procedural programming with its straightforward use of functions and flow control. It also supports object-oriented programming through its class system, which includes features like inheritance, encapsulation, and polymorphism. Additionally, Python's support for functional programming is robust, offering lambda functions, higher-order functions, and tools like map, filter, and reduce. This broad support allows developers to choose the paradigm that best fits the problem they are solving, or to blend paradigms to create more sophisticated solutions.

Community and Ecosystem:
Python's large and active community contributes to a rich ecosystem of libraries and frameworks that cater to various paradigms. Whether it's Django for object-oriented web

development, NumPy and Pandas for functional data processing, or Flask for procedural scripting, the Python ecosystem provides tools that align with different programming approaches. This vibrant community also means that developers have access to extensive resources, tutorials, and examples for working with Python in multiple paradigms.

Interoperability:

Python's ability to interface with other languages and systems enhances its multi-paradigm strengths. For instance, Python can easily integrate with C/C++ for performance-critical tasks (procedural), work with Java or .NET libraries for object-oriented programming, and interact with specialized functional programming languages through APIs or embedded systems. This interoperability ensures that Python can serve as a "glue" language, binding together different paradigms and technologies into a cohesive whole.

Python's excellence in multiple paradigms makes it an invaluable tool for developers. Whether you're developing a simple script, a complex web application, or a sophisticated data pipeline, Python's multi-paradigm support allows you to choose the right approach for the job, ensuring that your code is both powerful and maintainable. As you advance in your Python programming journey, this flexibility will enable you to tackle a wide range of challenges with confidence, leveraging the best aspects of each paradigm to create elegant and effective solutions.

OVERVIEW OF PYTHON'S VERSATILITY

Python's versatility is one of the primary reasons it has become one of the most popular programming languages in the world. Its ability to adapt to a wide range of programming tasks, from simple scripting to complex application development, makes it an essential tool for developers across diverse fields. This versatility is rooted in several key features and characteristics that enable Python to be effective in multiple domains and paradigms.

1. Multi-Paradigm Support
Python's flexibility in supporting various programming paradigms—procedural, object-oriented, and functional—is

a major contributor to its versatility. Developers can choose the most suitable approach for a given task, whether it's writing simple scripts using procedural programming, designing complex systems with object-oriented techniques, or employing functional programming for concise, data-driven operations. This multi-paradigm support allows Python to be used in different contexts, from building scalable web applications to processing large datasets.

2. Extensive Standard Library and Ecosystem

Python comes with a comprehensive standard library that includes modules and packages for virtually any task, from file handling and system operations to web development and scientific computing. This rich standard library minimizes the need for external dependencies, enabling rapid development. Additionally, Python's ecosystem of third-party libraries and frameworks further extends its capabilities. Libraries like Django and Flask make web development straightforward, while NumPy, Pandas, and TensorFlow provide powerful tools for data science and machine learning. This extensive ecosystem ensures that Python can be adapted to meet the needs of nearly any project.

3. Cross-Platform Compatibility

Python's cross-platform nature is another aspect of its versatility. Python code can be written and executed on various operating systems, including Windows, macOS, and Linux, with little to no modification. This makes Python an excellent choice for developing applications that need to run across different environments. Furthermore, Python's compatibility with other languages and systems allows it to integrate seamlessly with existing codebases and technologies, making it a powerful "glue" language in multi-language projects.

4. Ease of Learning and Use

Python's simple and readable syntax makes it an accessible language for beginners, while its powerful features appeal to experienced developers. This ease of use translates to faster development times and reduced learning curves, enabling developers to quickly prototype ideas and iterate on them. The language's emphasis on readability also means that Python code is easier to maintain and share, promoting collaboration and long-term project sustainability.

5. Strong Community and Support

Python's large and active community contributes significantly to its versatility. The community-driven development model ensures that Python continuously evolves to meet new challenges and trends in software development. The vast amount of documentation, tutorials, and forums available online provides resources for both beginners and advanced users, fostering a supportive environment for learning and problem-solving. Additionally, the community's contributions to open-source projects and libraries ensure that Python remains at the forefront of innovation in fields like web development, data science, and artificial intelligence.

6. Broad Applicability Across Domains

Python's versatility is evident in its widespread use across various industries and domains. In web development, Python is used to build everything from small websites to large-scale web applications. In data science, Python is the language of choice for data analysis, machine learning, and visualization. In automation, Python scripts are used to automate tasks, manage systems, and perform complex workflows. Python is also widely used in education, finance, scientific research, and even in emerging fields like quantum computing. This broad applicability makes Python an indispensable tool for developers working in diverse fields.

7. Scalability and Performance

While Python is known for its simplicity and ease of use, it is also capable of handling large-scale applications. With the right frameworks and optimization techniques, Python can be scaled to support high-performance applications, making it suitable for enterprise-level projects. Python's ability to interface with lower-level languages like C/C++ allows developers to optimize performance-critical parts of their applications, ensuring that Python remains a viable choice even in performance-sensitive environments.

In summary, Python's versatility lies in its ability to adapt to a wide range of programming needs, from simple scripts to complex, scalable applications. Its support for multiple paradigms, extensive standard library, cross-platform compatibility, ease of learning, and strong community all contribute to making Python a powerful and flexible language for developers across the globe. Whether you are building a quick prototype or a full-fledged system, Python's versatility ensures that it can meet the demands of your project efficiently and effectively.

Introduction to Python's Core Features

Python is celebrated for its simplicity and power, making it an ideal language for both beginners and experienced developers. At the heart of Python's success are its core features, which provide a robust foundation for a wide range of programming tasks. These features not only make Python easy to learn and use but also enable it to handle complex applications efficiently. Here's an introduction to some of Python's most essential features:

1. Simple and Readable Syntax

Python's syntax is designed to be clean and easy to read, resembling natural language to a greater extent than many other programming languages. This simplicity reduces the cognitive load on developers, allowing them to focus more on solving problems than on the intricacies of the language itself. Python's use of indentation to define code blocks, rather than braces or keywords, further enhances readability and enforces a consistent coding style.

2. Interpreted Language

Python is an interpreted language, meaning that code is executed line by line without the need for prior compilation. This allows for quick testing and debugging, as developers can run their code and see results immediately. The interactive Python interpreter also enables developers to experiment with code snippets in real time, making it a powerful tool for learning and prototyping.

3. Dynamic Typing

Python uses dynamic typing, which means that variables do not need to be explicitly declared with a type. Instead, the type of a variable is determined at runtime based on the value assigned to it. This flexibility allows for faster development and easier experimentation, as developers can quickly change variable types without altering large portions of their code. However, it also requires careful management to avoid type-related errors.

4. Automatic Memory Management

Python handles memory management automatically through a built-in garbage collector. This feature frees developers from manually allocating and deallocating memory, reducing the risk of memory leaks and other related bugs. Automatic memory management is particularly beneficial in large and complex applications, where manual memory handling can become error-prone and difficult to manage.

5. Extensive Standard Library

.One of Python's standout features is its extensive standard library, which provides modules and packages for a wide variety of tasks, including file I/O, system operations, web development, and data manipulation. The standard library is often described as "batteries included" because it equips developers with the tools they need to handle common programming tasks without relying on external libraries. This reduces the need to write code from scratch and speeds up development.

6. Cross-Platform Compatibility

Python is designed to be cross-platform, meaning that Python code can run on multiple operating systems, including Windows, macOS, and Linux, without modification. This makes Python an excellent choice for developing software that needs to be deployed across different environments. Python's compatibility with various platforms also extends to its ability to interface with other languages and systems, further enhancing its flexibility.

7. Support for Multiple Programming Paradigms

Python is a multi-paradigm language, supporting procedural, object-oriented, and functional programming. This allows developers to choose the most appropriate paradigm for their specific tasks or to combine paradigms to create more efficient and elegant solutions. Python's flexibility in this regard makes it suitable for a wide range of applications, from simple scripts to complex, large-scale systems.

8. Strong Community and Ecosystem

Python benefits from a large and active community that contributes to its continuous development and expansion. This community-driven approach ensures that Python remains up-to-date with the latest advancements in technology and software development. Additionally, the

Python ecosystem is rich with third-party libraries and frameworks, covering everything from web development and data science to machine learning and automation. This ecosystem allows developers to quickly find and use pre-built solutions for common tasks, further accelerating development.

9. Comprehensive Documentation and Learning Resources

Python's official documentation is thorough and well-organized, making it an invaluable resource for both beginners and experienced developers. In addition to the official documentation, the Python community has produced a vast array of tutorials, guides, and examples that cater to all levels of expertise. This wealth of learning resources makes it easier for new developers to get started with Python and for experienced developers to deepen their knowledge and skills.

10. Interactive and Modular Design

Python's interactive mode allows developers to test snippets of code on the fly, which is particularly useful for learning and debugging. Python's modular design, where code is organized into modules and packages, promotes code reuse and maintainability. Developers can import existing modules into their projects or create their own, making it easier to manage large codebases and collaborate on complex projects.

In conclusion, Python's core features are what make it such a versatile and powerful programming language. Its simple syntax, dynamic typing, extensive standard library, and support for multiple paradigms all contribute to its ease of use and adaptability. Whether you are building a simple script, a data-driven application, or a large-scale system, Python provides the tools and flexibility you need to succeed. As you continue to explore Python, you'll discover that its core features not only simplify the development process but also open up a world of possibilities for solving complex problems and creating innovative solutions.

CHAPTER 2
Setting Up Your Python Environment

Before diving into Python programming, it's essential to have a well-configured development environment. Setting up your Python environment correctly ensures that you can efficiently write, test, and run your Python code. Whether you're a beginner just starting out or an experienced developer working on complex projects, having the right tools and configurations in place is crucial for a smooth coding experience.

In this section, we'll guide you through the process of setting up your Python environment, covering everything from installing Python on your system to configuring your preferred code editor or integrated development environment (IDE). We'll also explore how to manage dependencies using virtual environments, which are essential for maintaining clean and organized projects.

By the end of this section, you'll have a fully functional Python environment tailored to your needs, allowing you to focus on writing code and building applications without unnecessary setup hurdles. Whether you're working on a simple script or a large-scale application, having the right environment in place will make your Python development more efficient and enjoyable.

INSTALLING PYTHON

To begin your Python programming journey, the first step is to install Python on your system. Python is available for a wide range of operating systems, including Windows, macOS, and Linux, and the installation process is straightforward. Whether you're installing Python for the first time or upgrading to the latest version, this guide will walk you through the steps to get Python up and running on your machine.

1. Choosing the Right Python Version

Python comes in two major versions: Python 2 and Python 3. Python 3 is the latest version and is recommended for new projects, as it includes numerous improvements and updates over Python 2, which is no longer supported. Before you start the installation, ensure you are downloading Python 3, specifically the most recent stable release, which can be found on the official Python website.

2. Installing Python on Windows

Step 1: Download the Installer
Visit the official Python website and download the latest Python 3 installer for Windows. The installer comes in two versions: one for 32-bit and one for 64-bit systems. Choose the appropriate version based on your system architecture.

Step 2: Run the Installer

Once the installer is downloaded, run it. The installer will give you the option to add Python to your system PATH. Make sure to check the box that says "Add Python to PATH" to ensure that you can run Python from the command line.

Step 3: Choose the Installation Type

You can choose between "Install Now" or "Customize Installation." The "Install Now" option installs Python with the default settings, which is suitable for most users. If you need to specify the installation directory or select optional features, choose "Customize Installation."

Step 4: Complete the Installation

After selecting your preferences, click "Install." The installer will copy the necessary files and set up Python on your system. Once the installation is complete, you can verify it by opening the command prompt and typing python --version. This command should display the installed Python version.

3. Installing Python on macOS

Step 1: Download the Installer
Similar to Windows, go to the official Python website and download the latest Python 3 installer for macOS.

Step 2: Run the Installer

Open the downloaded .pkg file and follow the on-screen instructions to install Python. The installer will handle all the necessary steps, including setting up Python and the associated tools.

Step 3: Verify the Installation

Once the installation is complete, open the Terminal and type python3 --version. This command will display the installed Python version, confirming that Python 3 is correctly installed on your macOS system.

4. Installing Python on Linux

Most Linux distributions come with Python pre-installed. However, these versions may not be the latest, so you might want to install or upgrade to the latest Python version.

Step 1: Update Package Lists

Open your terminal and update your package lists with the following command:

```sql
Copy code
sudo apt update
```

Step 2: Install Python
To install Python 3, use the following command:

Copy code
sudo apt install python3
This will install the latest available version of Python 3 on your system.

Step 3: Verify the Installation

After the installation is complete, verify it by typing python3 --version in the terminal. This will display the installed Python version.

5. Installing Python on Other Platforms

Python is also available for installation on other platforms such as Raspberry Pi, BSD systems, and mobile operating systems. The installation process may vary slightly, but generally follows the same principles: downloading the appropriate installer, running it, and verifying the installation. For specialized platforms, refer to the official documentation or community resources for detailed installation instructions.

6. Upgrading Python

If you already have an older version of Python installed and want to upgrade to the latest version, you can follow similar steps as described above. On Windows and macOS, the installer will guide you through the upgrade process. On Linux, you can upgrade Python using the package manager by running the appropriate upgrade commands.

7. Configuring the Python PATH

After installing Python, it's crucial to ensure that your system recognizes the Python executable. This is typically handled automatically during installation, especially if you checked the "Add Python to PATH" option. If not, you'll need to manually add Python to your system's PATH environment variable, allowing you to run Python from any command line interface.

8. Verifying Your Python Installation

To confirm that Python is installed correctly, open your command line interface (Command Prompt, Terminal, or similar) and type the following command:

```
css
Copy code
python --version
or
```

```css
Copy code
python3 --version
```

This should display the Python version you installed. If you encounter any issues, double-check the installation steps or consult the Python documentation for troubleshooting tips.

With Python successfully installed, you're now ready to start writing and running Python code. The next step is to set up a suitable development environment, including a text editor or an Integrated Development Environment (IDE), and to explore how to manage your Python projects efficiently using tools like virtual environments. This foundational setup will ensure you have a smooth and productive experience as you delve deeper into Python programming.

Choosing the Right Version

When starting with Python, one of the first decisions you'll need to make is which version of Python to install. Python is available in two major versions: Python 2 and Python 3. While both versions have been widely used over the years, it's essential to understand their differences to make an informed decision. Here's a guide to help you choose the right version for your needs.

1. Python 2 vs. Python 3

Python 2 was the dominant version for many years and is still used in some legacy systems. However, Python 3 is the current and future standard. Python 3 introduced several improvements and changes that are not backward-compatible with Python 2, leading to a gradual shift in the Python community towards Python 3.

Python 2

Legacy Support: Python 2 is no longer actively maintained or supported, with the official end of support being January 1, 2020. Despite this, some older applications and systems may still run on Python 2, so it's occasionally necessary to use this version for compatibility reasons.

Limited Future Development: No new features or updates are being added to Python 2. Developers are encouraged to upgrade to Python 3 to take advantage of ongoing improvements and support.

Python 3

Active Development: Python 3 is actively developed, with regular updates and new features being added. It's the recommended version for new projects and development, ensuring you have access to the latest advancements in the language.

Improved Features: Python 3 includes numerous enhancements over Python 2, such as better Unicode support, improved syntax, and more powerful libraries. These improvements make Python 3 more efficient, readable, and easier to use.

Compatibility with Modern Libraries: Most modern libraries and frameworks are designed for Python 3, and support for Python 2 in these libraries is increasingly rare. By choosing Python 3, you'll have access to a broader range of tools and resources.

2. Why Python 3 is the Best Choice

For most developers, Python 3 is the clear choice, especially for new projects. Here are some reasons why Python 3 is recommended:

Future-Proofing: Python 3 is the present and future of the Python language. By starting with Python 3, you ensure that your code will be compatible with future updates and developments in the Python ecosystem.

Improved Syntax and Features: Python 3's syntax is cleaner and more consistent than Python 2's, making it easier to write and maintain code. Features like f-strings for string formatting, the print() function, and the asyncio library for asynchronous programming are just a few examples of Python 3's modern capabilities.

Better Support for Unicode: Python 3 handles Unicode strings natively, making it easier to work with text in different languages and character sets. This is particularly important in today's globalized world, where applications often need to support multiple languages.

Wider Adoption and Community Support: The majority of the Python community, including libraries, frameworks, and educational resources, has moved to Python 3. This means better support, more tutorials, and a larger pool of developers to collaborate with when using Python 3.

3. When You Might Need Python 2

While Python 3 is generally the best choice, there are a few specific scenarios where Python 2 might still be necessary:

Maintaining Legacy Code: If you're working on an existing project that was built with Python 2, it may be more practical to continue using Python 2, especially if the project is large and complex. However, it's often advisable to consider migrating to Python 3 when possible to take advantage of modern features and ongoing support.

Compatibility with Older Systems: Some older systems or applications may only support Python 2. In such cases, using Python 2 might be necessary to ensure compatibility. However, this situation is becoming increasingly rare as more systems are upgraded to support Python 3.

4. Version Compatibility
One of the key differences between Python 2 and Python 3 is the lack of backward compatibility. Code written in

Python 2 may not work in Python 3 without modification. If you have existing Python 2 code that you need to run in a Python 3 environment, you can use tools like 2to3 to help convert Python 2 code to Python 3. Additionally, many resources are available to guide you through the process of porting Python 2 code to Python 3.

5. Checking Your System for Python Versions

Before installing a new version of Python, it's a good idea to check if Python is already installed on your system and, if so, which version. You can do this by opening a command line interface and typing:

css
Copy code
python --version
or

css
Copy code
python3 --version
This command will display the version of Python currently installed on your system. If an older version is installed, you

can decide whether to upgrade to the latest version of Python 3.

6. Installing Multiple Python Versions

In some cases, you may need to have both Python 2 and Python 3 installed on the same system, particularly if you are maintaining legacy code while also developing new projects. Most operating systems allow you to install multiple versions of Python side by side. On many Linux distributions and macOS, for instance, Python 2 and Python 3 can be accessed separately using the commands python2 and python3. On Windows, tools like pyenv can help you manage multiple Python versions and switch between them as needed.

7. Final Recommendation

For most users, especially those starting new projects or learning Python for the first time, Python 3 is the recommended choice. It offers a modern, efficient, and well-supported platform that is continually evolving with new features and improvements. By choosing Python 3, you align yourself with the future of the language and ensure that your skills and projects are compatible with the latest developments in the Python ecosystem.

In conclusion, while Python 2 may still be necessary for certain legacy applications, Python 3 is the best choice for most developers. Its improvements in syntax, features, and support make it the ideal version for both new and ongoing projects. As you set up your Python environment, starting with Python 3 will give you the best foundation for successful and future-proof development.

Setting Up Python on Different Platforms

Setting up Python on your system is a crucial step to start coding and developing applications. Python supports various operating systems, and the installation process may differ slightly depending on the platform you are using. Below is a guide for installing Python on different platforms: Windows, macOS, and Linux.

1. Setting Up Python on Windows

Step 1: Download the Installer

Visit the official Python website and download the latest Python 3 installer for Windows. You will find options for 32-bit and 64-bit versions. Choose the version that matches your system architecture.

Step 2: Run the Installer

Double-click the downloaded .exe file to launch the installer. On the first screen, check the box that says "Add Python to PATH." This ensures that you can run Python from the command line.
Click "Install Now" for a default installation or "Customize Installation" if you need to select specific features or an installation directory.

Step 3: Verify the Installation

Once the installation is complete, open the Command Prompt by typing cmd in the Windows search bar and hitting Enter.
Type python --version or python3 --version to check if Python was installed correctly. The command should display the installed Python version.

2. Setting Up Python on macOS

Step 1: Download the Installer

Go to the official Python website and download the latest Python 3 installer for macOS. This will be a .pkg file.

Step 2: Run the Installer

Double-click the .pkg file to start the installation process. Follow the on-screen instructions to install Python. The installer will set up Python and include the python3 executable.

Step 3: Verify the Installation

Open the Terminal application, which you can find in Applications > Utilities or by searching in Spotlight. Type python3 --version to confirm that Python is installed correctly. The command should show the version number of Python.

3. Setting Up Python on Linux

Step 1: Update Package Lists

Open the Terminal. Depending on your Linux distribution, you might need to update your package lists. Use the following command:

bash

Copy code

sudo apt update

Step 2: Install Python

For most Debian-based distributions (like Ubuntu), you can install Python 3 using:

bash

Copy code

sudo apt install python3

For other distributions like Fedora or CentOS, use:

bash

Copy code

sudo dnf install python3

or

bash

Copy code

sudo yum install python3

Step 3: Verify the Installation

After installation, check the Python version by typing:
bash
Copy code
python3 --version
This command should display the Python version installed on your system.

4. Additional Steps for All Platforms

Setting Up Pip

Pip is the package installer for Python, allowing you to install additional libraries and packages. It is included by default with Python 3 installations. To verify that pip is installed, you can run:
bash
Copy code
pip3 --version
If pip is not installed, you can install it manually by following the instructions on the pip installation page.

Installing Virtual Environments

Virtual environments help you manage dependencies and isolate project-specific packages. To install virtualenv, use pip:
bash
Copy code
pip3 install virtualenv

Create a new virtual environment by navigating to your project directory and running:
bash
Copy code
python3 -m venv myenv

Activate the virtual environment:
On Windows:
bash
Copy code
myenv\Scripts\activate
On macOS and Linux:
bash
Copy code
source myenv/bin/activate
Configuring Development Tools

Choose a code editor or IDE that suits your needs. Popular choices include Visual Studio Code, PyCharm, and Sublime Text. Ensure that your editor is configured to use the Python interpreter you've installed.

Install any additional plugins or extensions for Python development to enhance your coding experience.

Updating Python

Keeping Python updated ensures you have the latest features and security improvements. Check for updates periodically and follow the same installation steps to upgrade to the latest version.

In summary, setting up Python on Windows, macOS, and Linux involves downloading the appropriate installer, running it, and verifying the installation. Each platform has its specific steps, but the general process is similar. Once Python is installed, setting up pip, virtual environments, and a development tool will complete your setup, providing you with a fully functional Python development environment.

WORKING WITH VIRTUAL ENVIRONMENTS

.

Virtual environments are a crucial tool for managing Python projects efficiently and avoiding common issues related to dependency management. They allow you to create isolated environments for different projects, ensuring that each project has its own set of dependencies and libraries, independent of other projects and the system-wide Python installation.

In this section, we'll explore the concept of virtual environments, why they are important, and how to use them effectively. You'll learn how to create, activate, and manage virtual environments, as well as how to install and manage dependencies within these environments. This approach not only helps keep your projects organized but also prevents version conflicts and ensures that your development environment remains clean and consistent.

By the end of this section, you'll understand how to leverage virtual environments to streamline your Python development workflow, making it easier to handle multiple projects, collaborate with others, and maintain a stable development setup.

Why Virtual Environments Matter

Virtual environments play a critical role in Python development by offering a structured way to manage project dependencies and isolate project-specific configurations. Here's why virtual environments are essential:

1. Isolation of Dependencies

Virtual environments create isolated spaces for each project, ensuring that dependencies installed for one project do not interfere with those of another. This isolation is crucial for avoiding conflicts between different versions of libraries. For instance, if Project A requires version 1.0 of a library and Project B needs version 2.0, using a virtual environment for each project prevents version clashes and ensures that each project functions correctly with its required dependencies.

2. Preventing Global Pollution

Installing libraries globally can clutter the system Python environment with packages that are only relevant to specific projects. This can lead to a polluted global namespace, making it difficult to manage and troubleshoot dependencies. Virtual environments prevent this issue by containing project-specific libraries within their own directories, thus keeping the global Python environment clean and manageable.

3. Consistency Across Development and Production

Virtual environments help ensure that your development environment closely matches your production environment. By creating and using a virtual environment, you can manage and replicate the exact versions of libraries and dependencies that your application needs. This consistency reduces the likelihood of encountering issues when deploying your application to different environments or systems.

4. Simplified Dependency Management
.

Managing dependencies within virtual environments is straightforward. You can easily install, update, or remove packages specific to a project without affecting other projects. Tools like pip and pipenv make it easy to handle project dependencies and generate requirements files (requirements.txt or Pipfile) that document the exact packages and their versions needed for a project.

5. Enhanced Collaboration

When working in a team or collaborating on projects, virtual environments facilitate consistency and reproducibility. By sharing the requirements file, team members can recreate the exact environment needed for the project, ensuring that everyone works with the same set of dependencies. This reduces "it works on my machine" problems and fosters a smoother collaborative workflow.

6. Testing and Experimentation

Virtual environments are ideal for testing new packages or experimenting with different versions of libraries. You can create a separate environment to test new features or library updates without risking the stability of your main projects. Once you're satisfied with the results, you can integrate the changes into your primary environment.

7. Easy Cleanup and Maintenance
When a project is completed or no longer needed, you can simply delete its virtual environment without affecting other projects or the system Python installation. This ease of cleanup helps manage disk space and keeps your development setup organized and clutter-free.

In summary, virtual environments are vital for effective Python development, providing isolation, preventing global pollution, ensuring consistency, simplifying dependency management, and enhancing collaboration. By using virtual environments, you create a more controlled, reliable, and manageable development process, leading to smoother project development and deployment.

Creating and Managing Virtual Environments

Virtual environments are indispensable for Python development, providing a clean, isolated workspace for each project. Here's a comprehensive guide on how to create and manage virtual environments efficiently:

1. Creating a Virtual Environment

Creating a virtual environment is straightforward and involves a few simple steps. Here's how to do it:

Using venv (Python's Built-in Tool)

Open your Command Line Interface: Access your terminal (macOS/Linux) or Command Prompt/PowerShell (Windows).

Navigate to Your Project Directory: Use the cd command to move to the directory where you want to create your virtual environment.

bash
Copy code
cd path/to/your/project
Create the Virtual Environment:

bash
Copy code
python3 -m venv env
python3 specifies the Python version to use.
-m venv calls the venv module to create the environment.
env is the name of the virtual environment folder (you can choose any name you like).

Using virtualenv (Third-Party Tool)

Alternatively, you can use virtualenv, a third-party package that offers additional features.

Install virtualenv (if not already installed):

bash
Copy code
pip install virtualenv
Create the Virtual Environment:

bash
Copy code
virtualenv env
Here, env is the name of the environment directory.

2. Activating the Virtual Environment

Once the virtual environment is created, you need to activate it to use it. Activation ensures that any Python or pip commands you use operate within the virtual environment rather than the global Python installation.

On Windows:

bash

Copy code
```
env\Scripts\activate
```
On macOS and Linux:

bash
Copy code
```
source env/bin/activate
```

After activation, your command line prompt will change to show the name of the activated environment, indicating that you are working within it.

3. Installing Packages

With the virtual environment active, you can use pip to install packages. These packages will only be available within the virtual environment, leaving your global Python installation untouched.

Install Packages Using pip:

bash
Copy code
```
pip install package_name
```

You can also install multiple packages from a requirements.txt file:

bash
Copy code
pip install -r requirements.txt

4. Managing Dependencies

Generating a Requirements File:
To create a requirements.txt file listing all the installed packages and their versions, use:

bash
Copy code
pip freeze > requirements.txt
This file can be shared with others to replicate the exact environment setup.

Updating Dependencies:
To update packages, you can specify the package name with pip:

bash

Copy code
pip install --upgrade package_name
Removing Packages:
To uninstall a package, use:

bash
Copy code
pip uninstall package_name

5. Deactivating the Virtual Environment

When you're done working in the virtual environment, deactivate it to return to the global Python environment:

bash
Copy code
deactivate

6. Deleting a Virtual Environment
If you no longer need a virtual environment, you can delete its directory to remove it entirely. This action will not affect other projects or the global Python installation.

Delete the Virtual Environment Directory:

Simply remove the environment folder:

On Windows:
bash
Copy code
rmdir /s /q env
On macOS and Linux:
bash
Copy code
rm -rf env

7. Using Multiple Virtual Environments

For different projects, you can create and manage multiple virtual environments. Each environment operates independently, allowing you to switch between them as needed. Just remember to activate the appropriate environment before running commands related to that specific project.

.8. Advanced Tools

pipenv and poetry:
For more advanced dependency management, tools like pipenv and poetry offer additional features such as easier

dependency resolution, environment management, and project configuration. These tools integrate with virtual environments but provide enhanced functionality and a more streamlined workflow.

Example with pipenv:

```bash
Copy code
pip install pipenv
pipenv install package_name
pipenv shell
```

Example with poetry:

```bash
Copy code
pip install poetry
poetry new project_name
poetry add package_name
poetry shell
```

In summary, creating and managing virtual environments is a key practice in Python development, allowing you to maintain project isolation, manage dependencies effectively, and ensure a clean, organized development environment. By following these steps, you can streamline your development workflow and avoid common pitfalls associated with dependency management.

PART II: MASTERING OBJECT-ORIENTED PROGRAMMING

CHAPTER 3
Introduction to Object-Oriented Concepts

Object-Oriented Programming (OOP) is a programming paradigm centered around the concept of "objects," which are instances of classes. It offers a powerful and intuitive approach to software design by organizing code into modular, reusable components. This paradigm is foundational in many programming languages, including Python, and helps in managing complexity, improving code maintainability, and promoting reuse.

In this section, we will introduce the fundamental concepts of OOP, including classes, objects, inheritance, encapsulation, and polymorphism. Understanding these principles is crucial for building robust, scalable applications and for leveraging the full potential of object-oriented languages like Python.

You will learn how to define and use classes and objects, how to create hierarchies of classes through inheritance, and how to encapsulate data to protect it from unintended modifications. Additionally, we'll explore polymorphism and how it allows for flexible and dynamic code execution. By mastering these concepts, you will gain a solid foundation in object-oriented programming, enabling you to write cleaner, more efficient, and maintainable code.

WHAT IS OBJECT-ORIENTED PROGRAMMING?

Object-Oriented Programming (OOP) is a programming paradigm that revolves around the concept of "objects," which are instances of "classes." OOP aims to model real-world entities and their interactions in a way that enhances code organization, reuse, and scalability.

In OOP, objects represent data and the operations that can be performed on that data. These objects are created from classes, which serve as blueprints defining the properties (attributes) and behaviors (methods) that the objects will possess. The primary goal of OOP is to create software that mirrors real-world scenarios, making it easier to understand, design, and manage complex systems.

Key principles of OOP include:

Encapsulation: Bundling data and methods into a single unit, or class, and restricting access to some of the object's components. This helps in protecting the integrity of the data and hiding the internal implementation details.

Inheritance: Creating new classes that are based on existing classes, allowing for a hierarchical organization of classes and promoting code reuse. Inheritance enables a new class to inherit attributes and methods from an existing class, reducing redundancy.

Polymorphism: Allowing different classes to be treated as instances of the same class through a common interface, enabling objects to be used interchangeably. This flexibility enhances the ability to extend and modify code.

Abstraction: Simplifying complex systems by providing a simplified interface and hiding unnecessary details. Abstraction allows developers to focus on interactions at a high level without needing to understand the intricate workings of each component.

By adopting OOP principles, developers can create more modular, flexible, and maintainable code, making it easier to manage and scale applications over time. Understanding these fundamental concepts will provide a strong foundation for leveraging OOP effectively in your programming projects.

Understanding Classes and Objects

In Object-Oriented Programming (OOP), classes and objects are fundamental concepts that form the backbone of the paradigm. They allow developers to model real-world entities and their interactions in a structured and intuitive way.

Classes

A class is a blueprint or template for creating objects. It defines a set of attributes (data) and methods (functions) that the objects created from the class will possess. Classes encapsulate data and behavior, providing a way to group related functionalities together.

Key Aspects of Classes:

Attributes: These are variables defined within a class that represent the state or properties of an object. For example, a Car class might have attributes such as color, make, and model.

Methods: These are functions defined within a class that describe the behaviors or actions that objects of the class can perform. For instance, a Car class might have methods like start_engine() and drive().

Constructor (__init__ Method): This special method initializes the object's attributes when a new instance of the class is created. It sets up the initial state of the object.

Example of a Class in Python:

```python
Copy code
class Car:
    def __init__(self, color, make, model):
```

```
        self.color = color
        self.make = make
        self.model = model


    def start_engine(self):
            print(f"The {self.color} {self.make} {self.model}'s
engine is now running.")

    def drive(self):
            print(f"The {self.color} {self.make} {self.model} is
driving.")
```

Objects
An object is an instance of a class. It represents a specific realization of the class blueprint, with its own unique set of attribute values. Objects are created from classes and can interact with other objects and classes through their methods.

Key Aspects of Objects:

Instantiation: Creating an object from a class is called instantiation. It involves calling the class as if it were a function, passing any required arguments to the constructor.

State: The state of an object is defined by its attributes. Each object maintains its own state, which is independent of other objects created from the same class.

Behavior: The behavior of an object is defined by the methods of its class. Methods operate on the object's attributes and perform actions specific to that object.

Example of Creating and Using Objects:

```python
Copy code
# Creating an object of the Car class
my_car = Car(color="red", make="Toyota", model="Corolla")

# Accessing attributes
print(my_car.color) # Output: red

# Calling methods
my_car.start_engine()  # Output: The red Toyota Corolla's engine is now running.
my_car.drive()       # Output: The red Toyota Corolla is driving.
```

Summary

Classes provide a blueprint for creating objects, defining attributes and methods that encapsulate data and behavior.

Objects are instances of classes, with their own unique state and behavior based on the class definition.

Understanding classes and objects is essential for leveraging OOP effectively. They allow you to create modular, reusable code and model complex systems in a way that reflects real-world entities and interactions. By mastering these concepts, you can build more organized and maintainable software solutions.

Key Concepts: Inheritance, Polymorphism, Encapsulation

In Object-Oriented Programming (OOP), several key concepts enable developers to create modular, flexible, and reusable code. Three of the most fundamental concepts are inheritance, polymorphism, and encapsulation. Understanding these concepts is essential for designing robust and maintainable software systems.

1. Inheritance

Inheritance allows a new class (called a subclass or derived class) to inherit attributes and methods from an existing class (called a superclass or base class). This promotes code reuse and establishes a hierarchical relationship between classes.

Key Points:

Code Reuse: By inheriting from an existing class, a subclass can reuse the code defined in the superclass, reducing redundancy and making the codebase easier to maintain.

Hierarchical Relationships: Inheritance models real-world hierarchies. For instance, a Bird class might be a superclass, and Sparrow and Eagle could be subclasses, inheriting common attributes and methods from Bird.

Method Overriding: A subclass can provide a specific implementation of a method that is already defined in its superclass. This is known as method overriding and allows subclasses to tailor the behavior of inherited methods.

Example in Python:

```python
Copy code
class Animal:
    def speak(self):
        print("Animal speaks")

class Dog(Animal):
    def speak(self):
        print("Dog barks")

class Cat(Animal):
    def speak(self):
        print("Cat meows")

# Usage
dog = Dog()
dog.speak()  # Output: Dog barks
```

2. Polymorphism

Polymorphism allows objects of different classes to be treated as objects of a common superclass. It enables the same method to behave differently based on the object's class type, promoting flexibility and scalability.

Key Points:

Method Overriding: Polymorphism is often achieved through method overriding, where a subclass provides a specific implementation of a method defined in its superclass.

Dynamic Method Dispatch: At runtime, the correct method implementation is selected based on the object's class, allowing for dynamic behavior.

Uniform Interface: Polymorphism allows different objects to be used interchangeably if they share a common interface or superclass. This simplifies code and enhances flexibility.

Example in Python:

```python
Copy code
def make_animal_speak(animal):
```

```
  animal.speak()

# Usage
animals = [Dog(), Cat()]
for animal in animals:
  make_animal_speak(animal)
# Output:
# Dog barks
# Cat meows
```

3. Encapsulation

Encapsulation involves bundling the data (attributes) and methods (functions) that operate on the data into a single unit or class. It also involves restricting direct access to some of the object's components to protect the integrity of the data.

Key Points:

Data Hiding: Encapsulation hides the internal state of an object and only exposes a controlled interface for interacting with it. This prevents unauthorized access and modifications to the object's data.

Public and Private Access: Attributes and methods can be marked as public or private. Public members are accessible from outside the class, while private members are intended for internal use only and are usually indicated by a leading underscore.

Controlled Access: Encapsulation allows you to control how the internal data is accessed and modified through methods, often referred to as getters and setters.

Example in Python:

```python
Copy code
class BankAccount:
    def __init__(self, balance):
        self.__balance = balance  # Private attribute

    def deposit(self, amount):
        if amount > 0:
            self.__balance += amount

    def withdraw(self, amount):
        if 0 < amount <= self.__balance:
            self.__balance -= amount
```

```python
def get_balance(self):
    return self.__balance


# Usage
account = BankAccount(100)
account.deposit(50)
print(account.get_balance())  # Output: 150
```

Summary

Inheritance allows for code reuse and hierarchical relationships between classes, enabling subclasses to inherit attributes and methods from superclasses.

Polymorphism enables objects of different classes to be treated uniformly based on a common interface or superclass, allowing methods to behave differently depending on the object's class.

Encapsulation bundles data and methods within a class and restricts access to the internal state of the object, promoting data protection and controlled interaction.

.

These core concepts of OOP work together to create flexible, maintainable, and reusable code, making it easier to manage complex software systems and model real-world scenarios effectively.

DESIGNING OBJECT-ORIENTED APPLICATIONS

Designing object-oriented applications involves applying the principles of Object-Oriented Programming (OOP) to create well-structured, modular, and maintainable software solutions. The goal is to leverage the strengths of OOP—such as encapsulation, inheritance, and polymorphism—to build applications that are both efficient and easy to understand.

In this section, we will explore the process of designing object-oriented applications from initial concept to implementation. We will cover essential design principles, including class design, interaction between objects, and the use of design patterns to solve common problems. By focusing on these aspects, you'll learn how to create applications that are scalable, flexible, and aligned with best practices in OOP.

You will gain insights into how to:

Identify and Define Classes and Objects: Determine the core components of your application and define the classes and objects that will represent these components.

Establish Relationships and Hierarchies: Design how classes will interact and inherit from one another, ensuring a logical hierarchy that promotes code reuse and clarity.

Apply Design Patterns: Utilize proven design patterns to address recurring problems and improve the overall design of your application.

Ensure Maintainability and Scalability: Create a design that allows for future changes and expansion while maintaining code quality and organization.

By the end of this section, you will be equipped with the knowledge and techniques needed to design robust, object-oriented applications that are both effective and maintainable.

Best Practices for Structuring Classes

.

Structuring classes effectively is crucial for creating clean, maintainable, and scalable object-oriented applications. Here are some best practices for designing and organizing classes:

1. Single Responsibility Principle

Each class should have a single responsibility or concern. This means that a class should handle one aspect of the application's functionality and do it well. By adhering to this principle, you ensure that your classes are focused, easier to understand, and simpler to maintain.

Example:
Instead of having a User class that handles user data and also manages user authentication, split these responsibilities into User and Authenticator classes.

2. Keep Classes Small and Focused

Avoid making classes too large or complex. Large classes can become unwieldy and difficult to manage. Aim to keep classes small and focused on a specific task or set of related tasks.

Example:
If a class has many methods or attributes, consider refactoring it into smaller, more specialized classes.

3. Use Descriptive Naming
Choose clear, descriptive names for your classes and their members. Names should reflect the role and purpose of the class or method, making the code more readable and self-explanatory.

Example:

Use InvoiceGenerator instead of a generic name like Generator, to make it clear that the class is responsible for generating invoices.

4. Encapsulation and Data Hiding

Encapsulate data within classes and use private attributes and methods to protect the internal state. Expose only what is necessary through public methods. This ensures that the internal implementation details are hidden, reducing the risk of unintended interference.

Example:
Use private attributes for internal data and provide public getter and setter methods to access and modify this data safely.

5. Implement Interfaces and Abstract Classes

When designing classes that should follow a certain contract or template, use interfaces or abstract classes. These constructs define methods that must be implemented by subclasses, promoting consistency and flexibility.

Example:
Define an abstract class Shape with an abstract method draw(), and have concrete classes like Circle and Rectangle implement this method.

6. Favor Composition Over Inheritance
Use composition to build classes from other classes instead of relying solely on inheritance. Composition allows for greater flexibility and reduces tight coupling between classes.

Example:

Instead of having a Car class inherit from a Vehicle class, consider composing a Car class with an Engine class, allowing you to change the engine without modifying the Car class.

7. Implement Proper Initialization

Ensure that classes are properly initialized using constructors (__init__ methods). Initialize all necessary attributes and ensure that objects start in a valid state.

Example:

In a BankAccount class, initialize the account balance and account holder's details in the constructor.

8. Apply Design Patterns Wisely

Use design patterns where appropriate to solve common design problems. Patterns like Singleton, Factory, and Observer can help manage object creation, state management, and communication between objects.

Example:

Use the Singleton pattern to ensure that only one instance of a ConfigurationManager class exists throughout the application.

9. Document Your Classes

Provide clear documentation for your classes, including their purpose, attributes, methods, and usage examples. This helps other developers (or your future self) understand how to use and extend the class effectively.

Example:
Include docstrings for classes and methods to describe their functionality and parameters.

10. Avoid Excessive Coupling

Minimize dependencies between classes to reduce the impact of changes and enhance modularity. Classes should interact with each other through well-defined interfaces rather than directly accessing each other's internals.

Example:

If Order class needs to interact with Customer class, do so through methods or interfaces rather than directly accessing Customer's attributes.

Summary

By following these best practices, you can design classes that are well-structured, maintainable, and flexible. Focusing on single responsibility, clear naming, encapsulation, and appropriate use of design patterns will lead to cleaner and more effective object-oriented designs. Adhering to these principles will ultimately result in software that is easier to understand, extend, and maintain.

Avoiding Common OOP Pitfalls

Object-Oriented Programming (OOP) provides powerful tools for structuring and managing code, but it's easy to encounter pitfalls if principles aren't applied correctly. Here's a guide to avoiding common OOP pitfalls and ensuring that your code remains clean, maintainable, and effective.

1. Overusing Inheritance

Pitfall: Over-relying on inheritance can lead to complex and fragile class hierarchies that are difficult to manage and understand.

Avoidance: Prefer composition over inheritance. Use inheritance to model "is-a" relationships, but when classes need to work together, consider using composition or interfaces. This keeps your design flexible and avoids deep inheritance trees.

Example: Instead of creating a deep hierarchy of Vehicle subclasses (e.g., Car -> ElectricCar -> LuxuryElectricCar), use composition to combine Engine, Transmission, and Features into Car.

2. Ignoring Encapsulation

Pitfall: Exposing internal state or making attributes public can lead to unintended modifications and break the integrity of your objects.

Avoidance: Use private attributes and provide public methods (getters and setters) to access and modify them. This encapsulates the data and provides a controlled interface for interacting with it.

Example: In a BankAccount class, use private attributes for the balance and provide methods like deposit() and withdraw() to modify it safely.

3. Creating God Objects

Pitfall: A "God Object" refers to a class that has too many responsibilities or knows too much about other classes. This leads to a lack of cohesion and makes the class difficult to maintain.

Avoidance: Apply the Single Responsibility Principle. Break down large classes into smaller, focused classes each handling a specific aspect of the application.

Example: Instead of having a UserManager class that handles user authentication, profile management, and notifications, separate these responsibilities into Authenticator, ProfileManager, and Notifier classes.

4. Neglecting Design Patterns

Pitfall: Failing to use appropriate design patterns can result in reinventing solutions to common problems, leading to inefficient or convoluted code.

Avoidance: Familiarize yourself with design patterns and apply them where suitable. Patterns like Singleton, Observer, and Factory can provide well-established solutions to common design issues.

Example: Use the Factory pattern to create different types of notifications (e.g., Email, SMS) rather than hard-coding the creation logic in your notification classes.

5. Overcomplicating Interfaces

Pitfall: Creating overly complex interfaces or having too many methods in a single interface can make the system difficult to implement and understand.

Avoidance: Keep interfaces simple and focused. Design interfaces with a clear purpose and limit the number of methods to what's necessary for that purpose.

Example: If creating a PaymentProcessor interface, ensure it only includes methods related to payment processing, such as process_payment(), rather than mixing in unrelated methods.

6. Not Leveraging Polymorphism

Pitfall: Failing to use polymorphism can lead to code duplication and make the system less flexible.

Avoidance: Utilize polymorphism to handle different object types through a common interface or superclass. This promotes code reuse and simplifies the extension of functionality.

Example: Instead of writing separate code for handling different types of shapes (Circle, Rectangle), use polymorphism to handle all shapes via a common Shape interface with a draw() method.

7. Inconsistent Naming Conventions

Pitfall: Using inconsistent or non-descriptive names for classes, methods, or attributes can make the code harder to read and understand.

Avoidance: Follow consistent and descriptive naming conventions throughout your codebase. Names should clearly indicate the purpose and functionality of the classes and methods.

Example: Use CustomerRepository instead of a vague name like CustomerManager to clearly indicate that the class handles data persistence.

8. Ignoring Testing

Pitfall: Neglecting to test object-oriented code can lead to undetected bugs and integration issues, especially when refactoring or extending functionality.

Avoidance: Write unit tests for your classes and their methods. Ensure that you test different scenarios and edge cases to verify that your classes work as expected.

Example: Use testing frameworks like unittest or pytest to create tests for class methods, ensuring that they handle various input cases correctly.

9. Overloading Classes

Pitfall: Overloading classes with too many responsibilities or methods can lead to complex and unwieldy code.

Avoidance: Design classes with a clear focus and avoid adding unrelated methods or responsibilities. Consider refactoring large classes into smaller, more cohesive units.

Example: A Report class should handle report generation and formatting, but not also handle data retrieval or user interactions. Separate these concerns into different classes.

Summary

By avoiding these common OOP pitfalls, you can design cleaner, more maintainable, and effective object-oriented systems. Emphasizing proper use of inheritance, encapsulation, and polymorphism, along with applying best practices like design patterns and consistent naming conventions, will help you create robust and scalable applications.

CHAPTER 4
Advanced Object-Oriented Programming

Advanced Object-Oriented Programming (OOP) delves deeper into the principles and techniques that build on the foundational concepts of OOP, such as classes, objects, inheritance, and polymorphism. It explores sophisticated topics and practices that enable developers to create more robust, flexible, and maintainable systems.

In this section, we will examine advanced OOP concepts that enhance your ability to design complex software architectures. We will cover topics such as design patterns, metaprogramming, and the principles of solid object-oriented design. By leveraging these advanced techniques, you can tackle complex programming challenges, improve code reuse, and optimize application performance.

Key Areas of Focus:

Design Patterns: Learn about common design patterns like Singleton, Factory, Strategy, and Observer that provide proven solutions to recurring design problems and help manage software complexity.

Metaprogramming: Explore how to use Python's metaprogramming capabilities to write code that can modify itself or interact with classes and objects dynamically at runtime.

SOLID Principles: Understand the SOLID principles (Single Responsibility, Open/Closed, Liskov Substitution, Interface Segregation, and Dependency Inversion) that guide the creation of well-structured and maintainable object-oriented systems.

Advanced Inheritance Techniques: Discover techniques for managing multiple inheritance, using abstract base classes, and employing mixins to build flexible class hierarchies.

Decorators and Context Managers: Dive into Python's decorators and context managers to extend functionality and manage resources efficiently.

By mastering these advanced OOP techniques, you will enhance your ability to design scalable and efficient applications, handle complex use cases, and write clean, maintainable code that stands the test of time.

i

WORKING WITH INHERITANCE AND POLYMORPHISM

Inheritance and polymorphism are fundamental concepts in Object-Oriented Programming (OOP) that enable developers to create flexible and reusable code. These concepts allow you to build complex systems by extending existing classes and defining how different objects can interact through shared interfaces.

In this section, we will delve into the practical applications of inheritance and polymorphism, exploring how they can be effectively utilized to design and implement sophisticated software systems.

Key Areas of Focus:

Inheritance: Understand how to create subclass relationships to extend or modify the behavior of existing classes. Learn how to use inheritance to promote code reuse and simplify complex hierarchies.

Polymorphism: Explore how polymorphism allows objects of different types to be treated uniformly based on a common interface or superclass. Discover how polymorphic behavior can be achieved through method overriding and dynamic method dispatch.

Real-World Examples: Examine real-world scenarios where inheritance and polymorphism are applied to solve problems, such as designing extensible frameworks, managing diverse object types, and implementing flexible interfaces.

Best Practices: Learn best practices for applying inheritance and polymorphism to avoid common pitfalls such as deep inheritance trees and excessive coupling. Understand how to balance these concepts to achieve a maintainable and scalable codebase.

By mastering inheritance and polymorphism, you will gain the skills needed to create more adaptable and efficient object-oriented designs, making it easier to manage and extend your codebase as your application grows and evolves.

Designing Class Hierarchies

Designing effective class hierarchies is a critical aspect of Object-Oriented Programming (OOP), as it lays the foundation for how different components of your system interact and extend each other. A well-designed class hierarchy promotes code reuse, improves maintainability, and enhances the scalability of your application. However, creating a clear and logical hierarchy requires careful planning and adherence to key OOP principles.

1. Understand the Domain and Requirements

Before designing your class hierarchy, thoroughly understand the domain and the specific requirements of the system you're building. Identify the core entities and their relationships within the problem domain. This understanding will guide the creation of a hierarchy that reflects the real-world structure of the problem.

Example: In a transportation system, you might identify entities such as Vehicle, Car, Bicycle, and Truck, each with its own characteristics and behaviors.

2. Apply the Single Responsibility Principle

Ensure that each class in the hierarchy has a single responsibility. Classes should represent distinct entities or concepts, with each class focusing on a specific aspect of the system. This keeps the hierarchy clean and prevents any one class from becoming overly complex.

Example: Separate the responsibilities of a PaymentProcessor class from those of a TransactionLogger class, even if they are closely related in functionality.

3. Use Inheritance for "Is-a" Relationships

Inheritance should be used to represent "is-a" relationships where a subclass is a specialized form of a superclass. This allows subclasses to inherit common behavior and attributes from their parent class, reducing code duplication and promoting consistency.

Example: In a class hierarchy, Car might inherit from Vehicle, as a car is a type of vehicle and shares common attributes like speed and fuel_capacity.

4. Favor Composition Over Inheritance
While inheritance is useful, it can lead to rigid and overly complex hierarchies if overused. Favor composition over inheritance when a class should contain or use another class rather than extend it. Composition provides greater flexibility by allowing you to build complex functionality by combining simpler, modular classes.

Example: Instead of having a Car class inherit directly from an Engine class, use composition to include an Engine object within the Car class, allowing you to easily swap out different engine types.

5. Design for Extensibility
Create class hierarchies that can be easily extended in the future without modifying existing classes. This involves using abstract classes or interfaces to define common behavior, which can then be implemented by different

subclasses. This approach ensures that your hierarchy remains adaptable to new requirements.

Example: Define an abstract class Shape with an abstract method draw(), and let specific shapes like Circle and Rectangle extend this class and provide their own implementations of the draw() method.

6. Avoid Deep Inheritance Trees

Deep inheritance trees can make a class hierarchy difficult to understand and maintain. Each level of inheritance adds complexity and can introduce subtle bugs or unexpected behavior. Aim to keep the hierarchy shallow and use other techniques, such as composition, to manage complexity.

Example: Instead of creating a deep hierarchy like Vehicle -> Car -> ElectricCar -> LuxuryElectricCar, consider flattening the hierarchy and using composition to add specific features like electric or luxury components.

7. Implement Polymorphism Thoughtfully

Polymorphism allows objects of different classes to be treated as instances of the same class through a common interface. When designing class hierarchies, use polymorphism to enable flexible and interchangeable components. Ensure that subclasses adhere to the contract defined by their superclass or interface.

Example: If you have a PaymentMethod interface with methods like process_payment(), different payment types (e.g., CreditCard, PayPal) should implement this interface so they can be used interchangeably in the payment processing system.

8. Abstract Common Functionality

Identify common functionality across different classes and abstract it into a base class. This reduces redundancy and ensures that shared behaviors are consistently implemented across subclasses.

Example: In a graphics application, a Drawable base class could define common attributes like position and methods like draw(), which would be shared by all drawable objects like Circle, Rectangle, and Text.

9. Review and Refactor Regularly

As your application grows, periodically review and refactor your class hierarchy. Look for opportunities to simplify, reduce coupling, or improve the clarity of your design.

Refactoring helps to keep the hierarchy aligned with the evolving requirements of the system.

Example: If a Vehicle class starts to accumulate too many responsibilities, consider splitting it into more specialized classes like MotorVehicle and NonMotorVehicle, each with its own distinct hierarchy.

Summary
Designing class hierarchies is an essential skill in OOP that requires a balance between flexibility, clarity, and maintainability. By understanding your domain, applying key OOP principles like the Single Responsibility Principle, and using inheritance and composition wisely, you can create class hierarchies that are both powerful and adaptable. Regularly reviewing and refactoring your hierarchies ensures they remain effective as your application grows and changes.

Leveraging Polymorphism for Flexibility

Polymorphism is one of the cornerstones of Object-Oriented Programming (OOP) and plays a crucial role in creating flexible and maintainable software. By allowing objects of different classes to be treated uniformly through a common interface or superclass, polymorphism enables you to write more generic and reusable code. This flexibility is especially valuable in scenarios where the specific types of objects may vary but the operations performed on them remain consistent.

1. Understanding Polymorphism

Polymorphism allows different classes to implement the same interface or inherit from a common superclass, enabling objects of these classes to be treated as instances of the same type. The primary forms of polymorphism in Python are:

Subtype Polymorphism (Inclusion Polymorphism): Occurs when a subclass inherits from a superclass and can be used in place of the superclass. This is the most common form of polymorphism in OOP.

Parametric Polymorphism: Allows functions or methods to operate on objects of different types, typically achieved through generics or templates (though Python handles this more dynamically).

Ad-hoc Polymorphism (Overloading): Involves method overloading, where methods in a class can have the same name but differ in the type or number of parameters.

2. Implementing Polymorphism Through Inheritance
Inheritance is a key mechanism for implementing polymorphism. When a subclass inherits from a superclass, it can override or extend the behavior of the superclass's methods. This allows the subclass to be used interchangeably with the superclass in the context of the methods and properties defined in the superclass.

Example: Consider an application that processes payments. You might define a PaymentMethod superclass with a process_payment() method. Subclasses like CreditCardPayment, PayPalPayment, and BankTransferPayment can each implement the process_payment() method differently. However, all these subclasses can be treated as PaymentMethod objects, allowing the system to process payments uniformly without needing to know the specific payment type in advance.

```python
Copy code
class PaymentMethod:
    def process_payment(self, amount):
        raise NotImplementedError("This method should be overridden in subclasses")


class CreditCardPayment(PaymentMethod):
    def process_payment(self, amount):
        print(f"Processing credit card payment of {amount}")


class PayPalPayment(PaymentMethod):
    def process_payment(self, amount):
        print(f"Processing PayPal payment of {amount}")


class BankTransferPayment(PaymentMethod):
    def process_payment(self, amount):
        print(f"Processing bank transfer payment of {amount}")


def process_transaction(payment: PaymentMethod, amount: float):
    payment.process_payment(amount)


# All payment methods can be processed the same way
```

```python
payments = [CreditCardPayment(), PayPalPayment(), BankTransferPayment()]
for payment in payments:
    process_transaction(payment, 100.00)
```

In this example, the process_transaction() function can handle any PaymentMethod object, making it easy to extend the system with new payment types in the future.

3. Polymorphism Through Interfaces and Abstract Classes

Using interfaces (or abstract base classes in Python) further enhances polymorphism by enforcing a common set of methods that different classes must implement. This guarantees that any class adhering to the interface can be used interchangeably, increasing the robustness of your code.

Example: Define an abstract class Shape with an abstract method draw(). Concrete classes like Circle, Rectangle, and Triangle will implement the draw() method, allowing you to handle different shapes uniformly.

python
Copy code

```python
from abc import ABC, abstractmethod

class Shape(ABC):
    @abstractmethod
    def draw(self):
        pass

class Circle(Shape):
    def draw(self):
        print("Drawing a circle")

class Rectangle(Shape):
    def draw(self):
        print("Drawing a rectangle")

class Triangle(Shape):
    def draw(self):
        print("Drawing a triangle")

def render_shapes(shapes):
    for shape in shapes:
        shape.draw()

shapes = [Circle(), Rectangle(), Triangle()]
render_shapes(shapes)
```

Here, render_shapes() can take any list of Shape objects, demonstrating the power of polymorphism in simplifying code that needs to work with multiple types.

4. Dynamic Polymorphism

In Python, dynamic polymorphism allows for method overriding, where the method that gets called is determined at runtime based on the actual object type, not the reference type. This allows Python to provide even greater flexibility compared to statically-typed languages.

Example: If you have a base class Animal with a method speak(), and subclasses like Dog and Cat that override this method, calling speak() on an Animal reference will invoke the subclass's version of the method at runtime.

```python
Copy code
class Animal:
    def speak(self):
        pass

class Dog(Animal):
    def speak(self):
```

```
    print("Woof!")

class Cat(Animal):
   def speak(self):
      print("Meow!")

def make_animal_speak(animal: Animal):
   animal.speak()

animals = [Dog(), Cat()]
for animal in animals:
   make_animal_speak(animal)
```

This dynamic method dispatch allows Python to determine the correct method to execute at runtime, giving your code the flexibility to handle various object types seamlessly.

5. Benefits of Polymorphism

Code Reusability: Polymorphism allows you to write more generic and reusable code. A single function or method can operate on objects of different classes without knowing their exact types.

Extensibility: It's easy to extend your system by adding new classes that adhere to existing interfaces or inherit from base classes. The existing code doesn't need to change to accommodate new types.

Maintenance: Polymorphism promotes cleaner code by reducing the need for complex conditionals or type checks, making your code easier to maintain and refactor.

Flexibility: The ability to treat objects of different types uniformly provides flexibility in how systems are designed and evolved over time.

Summary
Polymorphism is a powerful tool in the OOP toolkit, allowing for the design of flexible, reusable, and maintainable systems. By leveraging polymorphism, you can create code that easily adapts to changes, handles new requirements without extensive refactoring, and simplifies interactions between different components of your application. Whether through inheritance, interfaces, or dynamic method dispatch, polymorphism enhances the versatility of your software, making it easier to manage complexity as your projects grow.

IMPLEMENTING DESIGN PATTERNS IN PYTHON

Design patterns are proven solutions to common software design problems that arise during the development process. They provide templates for solving recurring issues in a structured and efficient manner, helping developers create more robust, maintainable, and scalable applications. While design patterns are not unique to any particular programming language, Python's flexibility and dynamic nature make it particularly well-suited for implementing a wide range of design patterns.

In this section, we will explore how to implement various design patterns in Python, providing practical examples and insights into how these patterns can be used to address specific challenges in software development.

Key Areas of Focus:
Creational Patterns: Learn how to manage object creation in a way that enhances flexibility and reusability. We'll cover patterns like Singleton, Factory Method, and Builder, which help control the instantiation process and decouple client code from concrete classes.

Structural Patterns: Understand how to organize classes and objects to form larger structures while keeping these structures flexible and efficient. We'll dive into patterns like Adapter, Decorator, and Composite, which enable the creation of complex systems from simpler components.

Behavioral Patterns: Discover how to manage object interactions and define how responsibilities are distributed among objects. We'll explore patterns like Observer, Strategy, and Command, which facilitate communication and decision-making processes within your code.

Python-Specific Implementations: While design patterns are generally language-agnostic, Python's features—such as first-class functions, metaclasses, and dynamic typing—offer unique ways to implement and sometimes simplify traditional design patterns. We'll examine Python-specific idioms that enhance or replace standard patterns.

Why Use Design Patterns?
Reusability: Design patterns provide a blueprint for solving common problems, allowing developers to reuse well-established solutions rather than reinventing the wheel.

Scalability: Patterns help manage and reduce the complexity of large systems, making it easier to scale applications as they grow.

Maintainability: By following design patterns, developers can create code that is easier to understand, modify, and extend, leading to more maintainable software.

Communication: Design patterns serve as a common language among developers, improving collaboration and ensuring that teams can work together more effectively.

How to Approach Design Patterns

When implementing design patterns in Python, it's important to balance the theoretical aspects with practical application. Patterns should be used judiciously, applying them only when they genuinely add value to your design. Overuse of patterns can lead to unnecessary complexity, so understanding the problem you're trying to solve is key to selecting the appropriate pattern.

By mastering the implementation of design patterns in Python, you'll be able to enhance the structure and flexibility of your applications, making them more resilient to change and easier to extend. This section will provide you with the tools and knowledge to apply these powerful design principles in your own projects, ensuring that your codebase remains clean, efficient, and adaptable.

Exploring the Singleton Pattern

The Singleton pattern is one of the most well-known creational design patterns, used to ensure that a class has only one instance and provides a global point of access to that instance. This pattern is particularly useful in scenarios where a single instance of a class is needed to coordinate actions across a system, such as managing a connection to a database, maintaining a configuration object, or controlling access to a shared resource.

1. Understanding the Singleton Pattern

The core idea behind the Singleton pattern is to restrict the instantiation of a class to a single object. This means that no matter how many times you try to create an instance of the Singleton class, you will always receive the same object. This is achieved by controlling the object creation process within the class itself.

2. Implementing the Singleton Pattern in Python

Python, being a flexible and dynamic language, offers multiple ways to implement the Singleton pattern. Below are a few common methods:

Method 1: Using a Class Method
One simple approach to implement the Singleton pattern is by using a class method to manage the instance creation.

```python
Copy code
class Singleton:
    _instance = None

    @classmethod
    def get_instance(cls):
        if cls._instance is None:
            cls._instance = cls()
        return cls._instance

# Usage
singleton1 = Singleton.get_instance()
singleton2 = Singleton.get_instance()
```

```python
print(singleton1 is singleton2)  # Output: True
```
In this example, the get_instance() class method checks whether an instance already exists. If not, it creates one; otherwise, it returns the existing instance. This ensures that only one instance of the class is ever created.

Method 2: Using a Metaclass
A more Pythonic way to implement the Singleton pattern is by using a metaclass. Metaclasses allow you to control the creation of classes themselves, which can be leveraged to enforce the Singleton pattern.

python
Copy code
```python
class SingletonMeta(type):
    _instances = {}

    def __call__(cls, *args, **kwargs):
        if cls not in cls._instances:
            instance = super().__call__(*args, **kwargs)
            cls._instances[cls] = instance
        return cls._instances[cls]

class Singleton(metaclass=SingletonMeta):
```

```python
    def __init__(self):
        print("Singleton instance created")

# Usage
singleton1 = Singleton()
singleton2 = Singleton()

print(singleton1 is singleton2)  # Output: True
```

Here, the SingletonMeta metaclass overrides the __call__ method, which is responsible for creating new instances of a class. It checks if an instance already exists before creating a new one, thus ensuring the Singleton behavior.

Method 3: Using the __new__ Method
Another approach is to override the __new__ method, which is responsible for creating a new instance of the class before the __init__ method is called.

python
Copy code
```python
class Singleton:
    _instance = None

    def __new__(cls, *args, **kwargs):
```

```python
        if not cls._instance:
            cls._instance = super(Singleton, cls).__new__(cls,
*args, **kwargs)
        return cls._instance

    def __init__(self):
        print("Initializing Singleton instance")

# Usage
singleton1 = Singleton()
singleton2 = Singleton()

print(singleton1 is singleton2)  # Output: True
```

In this example, the __new__ method ensures that only one instance of the class is created, and subsequent calls return the existing instance.

3. Use Cases for the Singleton Pattern

The Singleton pattern is widely used in situations where a single point of control is needed:

Configuration Management: Applications often require a single configuration object that can be accessed and modified globally.

Logging: A single instance of a logger class ensures consistent logging throughout the application.

Database Connections: Managing a single connection to a database prevents the overhead and complexity of handling multiple connections.

Thread Pools: In multithreaded applications, a single instance of a thread pool can manage all threads, avoiding the complications of having multiple pools.

4. Considerations and Drawbacks

While the Singleton pattern can be useful, it's important to be aware of potential drawbacks:

Global State: Singleton instances can inadvertently introduce global state into an application, making it harder to manage and test. Overuse of global state can lead to hidden dependencies and bugs that are difficult to track down.

Testability: Singletons can make unit testing challenging because they introduce a shared state across tests, which can lead to flaky or hard-to-reproduce test failures. This is particularly problematic if the Singleton's state persists between tests.

Concurrency Issues: In a multithreaded environment, ensuring that a Singleton instance is created only once can be tricky and may require additional synchronization mechanisms.

Summary
The Singleton pattern is a powerful tool in a developer's arsenal, particularly when a single, centralized instance is required for managing shared resources or coordinating activities across an application. Python provides several ways to implement this pattern, each with its own advantages and trade-offs. However, like any design pattern, Singleton should be used judiciously, keeping in mind the potential drawbacks and ensuring it aligns with the overall design of the application. When applied correctly, the Singleton pattern can simplify the design of systems that require a single point of control, enhancing both the maintainability and clarity of your code.

Applying the Factory Method Pattern

The Factory Method pattern is a creational design pattern that provides an interface for creating objects in a superclass but allows subclasses to alter the type of objects that will be created. This pattern is particularly useful when a class can't anticipate the type of objects it needs to create, or when the responsibility for instantiating a particular object is better placed in a derived class.

1. Understanding the Factory Method Pattern
The Factory Method pattern delegates the process of object creation to subclasses. Instead of calling a constructor directly, you call a factory method, which will return an instance of a product class. This decouples the client code from specific classes, promoting flexibility and making the code easier to maintain and extend.

The key components of the Factory Method pattern are:

Product: The interface or abstract class defining the type of objects the factory method will create.

Concrete Product: The specific implementation of the product that is created by the factory method.

Creator: The class that declares the factory method, which returns an object of type Product. This is usually an abstract class or an interface.

Concrete Creator: Subclasses that implement the factory method to produce an instance of a specific Concrete Product.

2. Implementing the Factory Method Pattern in Python

Python's dynamic nature makes it particularly suited to the Factory Method pattern. Below is an example illustrating how the pattern can be implemented in Python.

Example: A Logistics System

Consider a logistics system where different types of transportation (e.g., Truck, Ship) are needed to deliver goods. Depending on the type of logistics, we might need to instantiate different transportation objects. The Factory Method pattern can help manage this complexity.

python

```python
Copy code
from abc import ABC, abstractmethod

# Product
class Transport(ABC):
    @abstractmethod
    def deliver(self):
        pass

# Concrete Products
class Truck(Transport):
    def deliver(self):
        print("Delivering by land in a truck.")

class Ship(Transport):
    def deliver(self):
        print("Delivering by sea in a ship.")

# Creator
class Logistics(ABC):
    @abstractmethod
    def create_transport(self) -> Transport:
        pass

    def plan_delivery(self):
```

```python
        transport = self.create_transport()
        transport.deliver()

# Concrete Creators
class RoadLogistics(Logistics):
    def create_transport(self) -> Transport:
        return Truck()

class SeaLogistics(Logistics):
    def create_transport(self) -> Transport:
        return Ship()

# Usage
if __name__ == "__main__":
    road_logistics = RoadLogistics()
    road_logistics.plan_delivery()  # Output: Delivering by
land in a truck.

    sea_logistics = SeaLogistics()
    sea_logistics.plan_delivery()  # Output: Delivering by sea
in a ship.
```

In this example:

Transport is the abstract Product class.

Truck and Ship are Concrete Products.

Logistics is the abstract Creator class that defines the factory method create_transport().

RoadLogistics and SeaLogistics are Concrete Creators that implement the factory method to return specific products.

3. Benefits of the Factory Method Pattern

Decoupling: The pattern decouples the client code from the concrete classes, promoting flexibility and reducing the dependency on specific implementations.

Single Responsibility Principle: The pattern adheres to the Single Responsibility Principle by isolating the object creation logic from the business logic, making the code easier to maintain.

Open/Closed Principle: The Factory Method pattern supports the Open/Closed Principle, as new product types can be added without modifying existing client code.

4. Use Cases for the Factory Method Pattern

Framework Development: The Factory Method pattern is commonly used in frameworks where the framework's core code needs to work with objects that are created by user-defined classes.

Plugin Architectures: When building a system that can be extended with plugins or modules, the Factory Method pattern allows for flexible instantiation of plugin classes.

Object Pooling: In scenarios where object creation is expensive, the Factory Method pattern can be used to manage a pool of reusable objects, returning existing instances instead of creating new ones.

5. Considerations and Drawbacks

While the Factory Method pattern is useful, it does come with some considerations:

Complexity: Introducing factory methods can add complexity to the code, especially if the number of product types and corresponding creators grows significantly.

Overhead: In some cases, using a factory method might introduce overhead if the pattern is applied to simple scenarios where direct instantiation would suffice.

Summary

The Factory Method pattern is a versatile and powerful design pattern that allows for the flexible creation of objects while adhering to key design principles such as decoupling, single responsibility, and open/closed. By implementing this pattern, you can make your codebase more adaptable to change, easier to extend, and more maintainable in the long run. Whether you're building a logistics system, a plugin architecture, or any other application where different types of objects need to be created dynamically, the Factory Method pattern can help you manage complexity and improve the overall design of your system.

PART III: FUNCTIONAL PROGRAMMING IN PYTHON

CHAPTER 5
Introduction to Functional Programming

Functional programming is a declarative programming paradigm that focuses on using pure functions and immutable data structures to build software. Unlike imperative programming, which emphasizes changing state and sequences of commands, functional programming revolves around composing and applying functions to achieve the desired outcomes.

In functional programming, functions are first-class citizens, meaning they can be passed as arguments, returned from other functions, and stored in data structures. This enables powerful abstractions like higher-order functions, which can manipulate other functions, and function composition, which allows you to build complex operations by combining simpler ones.

Key concepts include:

Pure Functions: Functions that always produce the same output for the same input and have no side effects.

Immutability: Data is never changed once created, reducing the risks associated with mutable state.

First-Class Functions: Functions are treated like any other variable, enabling flexible and reusable code.

Functional programming in Python, while not as strictly enforced as in languages like Haskell, is supported through features like lambda functions, map, filter, reduce, and comprehensions. Using these tools, you can write concise, maintainable, and bug-resistant code, especially in scenarios involving data transformations, concurrent tasks, or mathematical computations.

Pure Functions and Immutable Data

Pure functions and immutable data are foundational concepts in functional programming, offering significant benefits for code reliability, maintainability, and predictability.

Pure Functions

A pure function is a function that, given the same set of inputs, always produces the same output and does not cause any observable side effects. This means that a pure function's behavior is entirely determined by its inputs, and it doesn't alter any external state, making it predictable and easy to reason about.

Characteristics of Pure Functions:

Deterministic: For any given input, a pure function will always return the same output. This determinism makes testing and debugging more straightforward, as the function's behavior is consistent.

No Side Effects: Pure functions do not modify any external state or interact with the outside world (e.g., no modifying global variables, no I/O operations). The absence of side effects means that pure functions won't inadvertently alter the state of your program, reducing the risk of bugs.

Referential Transparency: Pure functions exhibit referential transparency, meaning that a function call can be replaced with its output value without changing the program's behavior. This property allows for more aggressive optimizations and easier reasoning about code.

Example of a Pure Function:
python
Copy code
```python
def add(a, b):
    return a + b

result = add(2, 3)  # Output will always be 5, regardless of
```
any external factors.

Here, add is a pure function because it always returns the same result for the same inputs and does not modify any external state.

Immutable Data

Immutability refers to the concept where data, once created, cannot be changed. Instead of modifying existing data, operations on immutable data structures return new instances with the updated values, leaving the original data unchanged. This approach reduces the complexity associated with state management and helps prevent unintended side effects.

Benefits of Immutability:

Predictability: Since data cannot be modified after creation, you can be confident that its value will remain consistent throughout the program. This consistency simplifies debugging and reasoning about the code.

Thread Safety: Immutability is inherently thread-safe, as multiple threads can read the same data without the risk of conflicts or race conditions, making it particularly useful in concurrent programming.

Simpler State Management: With immutable data, tracking and managing state changes becomes easier, as the state does not change in unexpected ways. This leads to more predictable and maintainable code.

Example of Immutable Data:
python
Copy code

```
# Immutable tuple
coordinates = (10, 20)

# Attempting to change the tuple will result in an error
# coordinates[0] = 15  # This would raise a TypeError

# Instead, you create a new tuple
new_coordinates = (15, 20)
```

In this example, coordinates is an immutable tuple. Instead of modifying it, we create a new tuple new_coordinates with the updated value.

Combining Pure Functions and Immutability

When combined, pure functions and immutable data provide a powerful foundation for building robust and maintainable software. Since pure functions don't modify external state and immutable data structures cannot be altered, the interactions between functions and data become much simpler and more predictable. This leads to fewer bugs, easier testing, and more reliable code.

For instance, consider a functional approach to manipulating a list of numbers:

python
Copy code

```python
def increment_all(numbers):
    return [x + 1 for x in numbers]

original_list = [1, 2, 3]
new_list = increment_all(original_list)

# original_list remains unchanged: [1, 2, 3]
# new_list is a new list with incremented values: [2, 3, 4]
```

Here, the increment_all function is pure and works with immutable data. It doesn't alter the original list but instead returns a new list with incremented values, preserving the integrity of the original data.

Summary
Pure functions and immutable data are central to functional programming, offering predictability, simplicity, and safety in software development. By adhering to these principles, developers can create code that is easier to reason about, less prone to bugs, and more resilient to changes. In Python, while not mandatory, adopting these practices can

significantly improve the quality and maintainability of your code, particularly in complex or concurrent applications.

Understanding Higher-Order Functions

Higher-order functions are a powerful feature in functional programming, allowing for a high degree of flexibility and reusability in your code. A higher-order function is defined as any function that either takes one or more functions as arguments, returns a function as its result, or both. This ability to manipulate functions as first-class citizens opens up a wide range of programming techniques that can lead to more concise, expressive, and maintainable code.

1. Key Characteristics of Higher-Order Functions

Higher-order functions are characterized by their ability to:

Accept Functions as Arguments: They can take other functions as parameters, enabling more abstract and general-purpose operations. For instance, instead of writing a loop to apply a certain operation to a list of items, you can pass a function to a higher-order function that handles the iteration and application.

Return Functions as Results: They can return new functions, allowing you to create customized behavior dynamically. This is particularly useful for building decorators, currying, or function factories.

2. Common Examples of Higher-Order Functions in Python

Python provides several built-in higher-order functions that you may already be familiar with, including map, filter, and reduce.

Map Function
The map function applies a given function to each item of an iterable (like a list) and returns an iterator with the results.

python
Copy code
```
def square(x):
    return x * x
```

```python
numbers = [1, 2, 3, 4]
squared_numbers = map(square, numbers)

print(list(squared_numbers)) # Output: [1, 4, 9, 16]
```
In this example, map is a higher-order function because it takes the square function as an argument and applies it to each item in the numbers list.

Filter Function
The filter function constructs an iterator from elements of an iterable for which a specified function returns True.

python
Copy code
```python
def is_even(x):
    return x % 2 == 0

numbers = [1, 2, 3, 4]
even_numbers = filter(is_even, numbers)

print(list(even_numbers)) # Output: [2, 4]
```
Here, filter is a higher-order function because it takes the is_even function and applies it to filter the numbers list, returning only the even numbers.

Reduce Function

The reduce function, which is part of the functools module, applies a rolling computation to sequential pairs of values in an iterable, ultimately reducing the iterable to a single cumulative result.

python
Copy code
```python
from functools import reduce

def add(x, y):
    return x + y

numbers = [1, 2, 3, 4]
sum_of_numbers = reduce(add, numbers)

print(sum_of_numbers) # Output: 10
```
In this case, reduce is a higher-order function because it takes the add function and applies it cumulatively to the numbers list, resulting in the sum of all elements.

3. Creating Custom Higher-Order Functions

Beyond using Python's built-in higher-order functions, you can also create your own to encapsulate reusable patterns or behaviors.

Example: Function Wrapper

Suppose you want to create a logging decorator that logs the execution of a function.

python
Copy code
```python
def logger(func):
    def wrapper(*args, **kwargs):
        print(f"Running {func.__name__} with arguments {args} and {kwargs}")
        result = func(*args, **kwargs)
        print(f"{func.__name__} returned {result}")
        return result
    return wrapper


@logger
def add(x, y):
    return x + y


add(2, 3)
```

Here, logger is a higher-order function because it takes the function add as an argument, wraps it with additional logging behavior, and returns the wrapped function. When add(2, 3) is called, the logging behavior is executed before and after the original function runs.

Example: Function Factory
You can also use higher-order functions to generate new functions based on parameters.

```python
Copy code
def multiplier(factor):
    def multiply_by_factor(x):
        return x * factor
    return multiply_by_factor

double = multiplier(2)
triple = multiplier(3)

print(double(5))  # Output: 10
print(triple(5))  # Output: 15
```

In this example, multiplier is a higher-order function that generates and returns new functions like double and triple, which multiply a given number by the specified factor.

4. Benefits of Higher-Order Functions

Using higher-order functions provides several advantages:

Code Reusability: Higher-order functions allow you to write more generic and reusable code. Instead of duplicating logic for different tasks, you can abstract the common parts into higher-order functions.

Modularity: They promote modularity by separating the concerns of what to do (the function passed as an argument) and how to do it (the higher-order function's implementation).

Simplified Code: Higher-order functions can often replace complex loops or conditionals with more concise and readable expressions.

Function Composition: They enable function composition, where you can build complex functionality by combining simpler functions.

Summary
Higher-order functions are a core concept in functional programming that greatly enhance the flexibility and expressiveness of your code. By understanding and utilizing them, you can write more modular, reusable, and

maintainable Python programs. Whether you're applying built-in functions like map, filter, and reduce, or crafting your own, higher-order functions help elevate your programming skills by abstracting patterns and promoting clean, elegant code.

LEVERAGING LAMBDA FUNCTIONS AND MAP/REDUCE

In functional programming, lambda functions and the map and reduce operations are powerful tools that streamline data processing and transformation. These features emphasize the functional programming paradigm's focus on concise, readable, and expressive code.

Lambda Functions

Lambda functions are anonymous functions defined using the lambda keyword in Python. They allow for the creation of small, throwaway functions that are typically used for short, simple operations where defining a full function might be unnecessary. Lambda functions are ideal for scenarios where you need a function for a brief period and don't want to formally define it using a def statement.

Map and Reduce

The map and reduce functions are built-in higher-order functions that apply a function to a sequence of items, enabling efficient and expressive data manipulation.

Map: The map function applies a given function to each item of an iterable, returning an iterator with the results. It's particularly useful for transforming data without needing to write explicit loops.

Reduce: The reduce function, available in the functools module, applies a function cumulatively to the items of an iterable, reducing the iterable to a single result. This is useful for combining data elements in a cumulative manner.

Together, lambda functions and map/reduce facilitate functional programming techniques that enable you to perform complex data transformations and aggregations with minimal and highly readable code.

Using Lambda Functions for Concise Code

Lambda functions, also known as anonymous functions, provide a way to write small, single-expression functions without the need for a full def block. They are defined using the lambda keyword and are particularly useful for scenarios where a short, one-off function is needed. Lambda functions enhance code readability and efficiency by reducing the boilerplate associated with standard function definitions.

Syntax and Structure
The basic syntax of a lambda function is:

```python
Copy code
lambda arguments: expression
```

lambda is the keyword that denotes the start of a lambda function.

arguments are the input parameters to the function.

expression is a single expression that the lambda function evaluates and returns.

Examples of Lambda Functions

1. Simple Operations

Lambda functions are often used for simple operations where a full function definition might be overkill.

```python
Copy code
# Lambda function to add two numbers
add = lambda x, y: x + y
print(add(5, 3))  # Output: 8
```

In this example, the lambda function lambda x, y: x + y performs a basic addition and is assigned to the variable add. This allows you to use add just like any other function.

2. Sorting and Filtering

Lambda functions are frequently used with sort, filter, and map functions for concise and readable data manipulation.

```python
Copy code
# Sorting a list of tuples by the second element
```

```
data = [(1, 'apple'), (2, 'banana'), (3, 'cherry')]
sorted_data = sorted(data, key=lambda x: x[1])
print(sorted_data)  # Output: [(1, 'apple'), (2, 'banana'), (3,
'cherry')]
```

Here, lambda x: x[1] is used as the key function for sorting the list of tuples based on the second element.

3. Mapping Values

Lambda functions are often used with map to apply a function to each item in an iterable.

```python
Copy code
numbers = [1, 2, 3, 4]
squared_numbers = map(lambda x: x ** 2, numbers)
print(list(squared_numbers))  # Output: [1, 4, 9, 16]
```

In this example, lambda x: x ** 2 is used to square each number in the numbers list.

4. Filtering Data

Lambda functions can be combined with filter to extract elements from an iterable based on a condition.

python
Copy code

```python
numbers = [1, 2, 3, 4, 5]
even_numbers = filter(lambda x: x % 2 == 0, numbers)
print(list(even_numbers))  # Output: [2, 4]
```

Here, lambda x: x % 2 == 0 filters out only the even numbers from the numbers list.

Advantages of Lambda Functions

Conciseness: Lambda functions allow you to define simple functions in a single line of code, which is particularly useful for short-lived or throwaway functions.

Readability: By avoiding the boilerplate of a full function definition, lambda functions can make your code more readable and focused on the task at hand.

Functional Programming Integration: Lambda functions work seamlessly with higher-order functions like map, filter, and reduce, enabling expressive and functional-style programming.

Limitations of Lambda Functions

While lambda functions offer concise syntax, they also have limitations:

Single Expression: Lambda functions can only contain a single expression, which limits their complexity. They cannot include statements, multiple expressions, or complex logic.

Readability: Overuse of lambda functions, especially for complex logic, can sometimes lead to code that is harder to read and understand.

Summary
Lambda functions are a powerful feature in Python that enable you to write concise, inline functions for simple operations. They are especially useful in functional programming contexts, such as when working with map, filter, and reduce. While they simplify code by reducing boilerplate, it is important to use them judiciously to maintain code readability and clarity.

Mapping, Reducing, and Filtering Data Efficiently

Mapping, reducing, and filtering are fundamental techniques in functional programming that allow you to process and manipulate data efficiently. These techniques, supported by Python's built-in functions and lambda expressions, enable you to perform complex operations with concise and readable code.

Mapping Data

Mapping is the process of applying a function to each item in an iterable (such as a list or a tuple) to produce a new iterable with the transformed items. The map function in Python is used to accomplish this.

How It Works:

Function: A function is applied to each element of the iterable.

Iterable: The source iterable containing elements to be transformed.

Result: An iterator yielding the results of applying the function.

Example:
python

Copy code
```
numbers = [1, 2, 3, 4]
squared_numbers = map(lambda x: x ** 2, numbers)
print(list(squared_numbers)) # Output: [1, 4, 9, 16]
```
In this example, lambda x: x ** 2 is applied to each element of the numbers list, resulting in a new list where each number is squared.

Reducing Data

Reducing involves applying a function cumulatively to the items of an iterable, reducing the iterable to a single cumulative result. The reduce function from the functools module is used for this purpose.

How It Works:
Function: A function is applied iteratively to pairs of items in the iterable.
Iterable: The source iterable to be reduced.
Result: A single value resulting from the cumulative application of the function.

Example:
python
Copy code

```
from functools import reduce

numbers = [1, 2, 3, 4]
sum_of_numbers = reduce(lambda x, y: x + y, numbers)
print(sum_of_numbers) # Output: 10
```
Here, lambda x, y: x + y is used to cumulatively add the numbers in the list, resulting in their total sum.

Filtering Data

Filtering involves selecting elements from an iterable based on a condition, creating a new iterable with only those elements that satisfy the condition. The filter function is used for filtering.

How It Works:

Function: A function that returns True or False for each item in the iterable.
Iterable: The source iterable to be filtered.
Result: An iterator containing only the elements that satisfy the condition.
Example:
python
Copy code

```python
numbers = [1, 2, 3, 4, 5]
even_numbers = filter(lambda x: x % 2 == 0, numbers)
print(list(even_numbers)) # Output: [2, 4]
```

In this case, lambda x: x % 2 == 0 is used to filter out only the even numbers from the list.

Combining Map, Reduce, and Filter

These techniques can be combined to perform complex data transformations efficiently. For example, you might first filter data to include only relevant elements, then map a transformation function to those elements, and finally reduce the result to a summary value.

Example:
python
Copy code

```python
from functools import reduce

numbers = [1, 2, 3, 4, 5, 6]
result = reduce(
    lambda x, y: x + y,
        map(lambda x: x ** 2, filter(lambda x: x % 2 == 0,
numbers))
)
```

```
print(result)  # Output: 56 (i.e., 4^2 + 6^2)
```

In this example:

filter(lambda x: x % 2 == 0, numbers) filters out even numbers.
map(lambda x: x ** 2, ...) squares each of the filtered numbers.
reduce(lambda x, y: x + y, ...) sums up the squared numbers.

Benefits of Mapping, Reducing, and Filtering

Efficiency: These operations are optimized for performance and can handle large datasets effectively.
Conciseness: They allow for more compact code compared to traditional loops and conditionals.
Readability: The functional programming style often leads to clearer and more expressive code.

Summary

Mapping, reducing, and filtering are essential techniques in functional programming that enable efficient data processing and transformation. By leveraging Python's map, reduce, and filter functions, along with lambda expressions, you can write concise and expressive code that handles data manipulation tasks effectively. These techniques not only simplify your code but also enhance its performance and readability.

CHAPTER 6
Advanced Functional Programming Techniques

Advanced functional programming techniques build on the foundational principles of functional programming to handle more complex scenarios and enhance code efficiency and flexibility. These techniques enable developers to write highly modular, reusable, and expressive code by leveraging advanced constructs and patterns. They are particularly valuable for solving intricate problems with elegant, concise solutions.

Key Areas of Focus

Function Composition: Combining multiple functions to create complex operations from simpler ones. This technique enhances code modularity and reuse by allowing you to build complex behaviors through the composition of smaller, well-defined functions.

Currying and Partial Application: Transforming functions to handle arguments in a more flexible way. Currying involves breaking down a function that takes multiple arguments into a series of functions, each taking a single argument. Partial application allows you to fix a number of arguments of a function and produce a new function.

Memoization: Storing the results of expensive function calls and reusing them when the same inputs occur again. Memoization improves performance by avoiding redundant computations, especially in scenarios with repeated function calls with the same arguments.

Higher-Order Functions: Using functions that take other functions as arguments or return functions as results. This includes patterns like decorators and function factories that enable dynamic behavior and reusable function logic.

Immutable Data Structures: Working with data structures that do not change after creation. Immutable data structures ensure that data is not modified accidentally, which simplifies reasoning about code and enhances functional programming principles.

Monads and Functors: Advanced abstractions used to manage side effects and handle operations in a functional context. Monads provide a way to sequence computations, while functors allow for mapping functions over data structures in a consistent manner.

Importance of Advanced Techniques

Advanced functional programming techniques help tackle complex programming challenges with greater clarity and efficiency. They promote code that is not only cleaner and more modular but also more maintainable and scalable. By applying these techniques, developers can create robust applications that leverage the full power of functional programming.

USING DECORATORS FOR FUNCTIONALITY ENHANCEMENT

Decorators are a powerful feature in Python that allow you to extend or modify the behavior of functions or methods dynamically and elegantly. By wrapping a function with additional functionality, decorators provide a clean and reusable way to enhance or alter behavior without modifying the original function's code. This capability makes decorators a key tool in functional programming and software design.

What are Decorators?

In Python, a decorator is a design pattern that allows you to "decorate" or "wrap" a function with additional functionality. It is implemented as a higher-order function that takes another function as an argument and returns a new function with the enhanced or altered behavior. Decorators are commonly used to add features such as logging, access control, memoization, and performance monitoring to functions or methods.

Why Use Decorators?

Separation of Concerns: Decorators help keep code modular by separating the concerns of different functionalities. This means you can add features to functions without cluttering their core logic.

Reusability: Once defined, decorators can be applied to multiple functions, promoting code reuse and consistency across your codebase.

Readability: Decorators enhance readability by clearly indicating the purpose and effect of the additional functionality applied to a function.

Flexibility: They allow for dynamic enhancement of functions, making it easier to apply changes and upgrades to your codebase.

How Decorators Work

Decorators are implemented as functions (or classes) that return a new function. They are applied using the @decorator_name syntax above the function definition. This syntax is syntactic sugar that simplifies the application of decorators and makes the code more readable.

Example: Basic Decorator
Here's a simple example of a decorator that logs the execution of a function:

```python
Copy code
def logger(func):
    def wrapper(*args, **kwargs):
```

```
    print(f"Calling {func.__name__} with arguments
{args} and {kwargs}")
    result = func(*args, **kwargs)
    print(f"{func.__name__} returned {result}")
    return result
  return wrapper


@logger
def add(x, y):
  return x + y


add(5, 3)
```

In this example, the logger decorator wraps the add function, logging its arguments and return value every time it is called.

Summary

Using decorators for functionality enhancement provides a robust mechanism for adding features and modifying behavior in a clean and modular way. They allow developers to maintain separation of concerns, enhance code readability, and promote reuse, all while preserving the integrity of the original function logic.

Understanding Decorator Patterns

The Decorator Pattern is a structural design pattern that allows you to add new functionality to an object dynamically without altering its structure. This pattern is widely used in software development to enhance the behavior of objects in a flexible and reusable manner. In Python, decorators leverage this pattern to modify or extend the behavior of functions or methods.

Key Concepts of the Decorator Pattern

Base Component: This is the core functionality or interface that defines the object's basic behavior. In Python, this would be the original function or method that you want to enhance.

Decorator: A decorator is a wrapper that adds additional functionality to the base component. It implements the same interface as the base component, ensuring compatibility and allowing the original object to be used interchangeably with the decorated version.

Concrete Decorator: This is a specific implementation of a decorator that adds a particular feature or behavior.

Multiple concrete decorators can be used in combination to achieve complex functionalities.

Client: The client uses the base component and the decorators to achieve the desired behavior. It interacts with the component through the decorator interface, without needing to know the details of the enhancement.

How the Decorator Pattern Works

The Decorator Pattern is implemented by creating a decorator class or function that wraps the base component. The decorator typically has a __call__ method (in the case of a function-based decorator) or a method (in the case of a class-based decorator) that extends the behavior of the base component while preserving its original interface.

Example: Function-Based Decorators
In Python, decorators are often implemented as functions that take another function as an argument and return a new function. Here's a simple example of a decorator pattern using function-based decorators:

python
Copy code

```python
def uppercase_decorator(func):
    def wrapper(*args, **kwargs):
        result = func(*args, **kwargs)
        return result.upper()
    return wrapper

@uppercase_decorator
def greet(name):
    return f"Hello, {name}"

print(greet("Alice"))  # Output: HELLO, ALICE
```

In this example, uppercase_decorator is a decorator that transforms the result of the greet function to uppercase.

Example: Class-Based Decorators

Class-based decorators use classes to implement the decorator pattern. The class defines a __call__ method that allows an instance of the class to be used as a decorator.

```python
python
Copy code
class RepeatDecorator:
    def __init__(self, times):
```

```python
        self.times = times

    def __call__(self, func):
        def wrapper(*args, **kwargs):
            result = func(*args, **kwargs)
            return [result] * self.times
        return wrapper

@RepeatDecorator(times=3)
def get_message(message):
    return message

print(get_message("Hello"))   # Output: ['Hello', 'Hello',
'Hello']
```

Here, RepeatDecorator is a class-based decorator that repeats the result of the get_message function a specified number of times.

Advantages of the Decorator Pattern

Enhanced Flexibility: Allows adding and removing functionalities dynamically at runtime without altering the original object or class.

Open/Closed Principle: Follows the principle of keeping software entities open for extension but closed for modification. Decorators can be added to extend behavior without changing existing code.

Single Responsibility Principle: Each decorator handles a specific aspect of functionality, adhering to the principle of having one reason to change.

Composability: Multiple decorators can be combined to build complex behaviors from simpler components, facilitating modular design.

Use Cases

Logging: Adding logging capabilities to functions or methods to track their usage and behavior.
Access Control: Implementing authentication or authorization checks before allowing access to certain functionality.
Caching: Enhancing performance by caching results of expensive function calls.
Validation: Adding input validation or preprocessing to ensure data integrity.

Summary

The Decorator Pattern is a versatile design pattern that enables dynamic and flexible enhancement of object behavior. By wrapping base components with decorators, you can add new functionality while adhering to the original interface. This pattern promotes modularity, reuse, and adherence to key design principles, making it a valuable tool in software development.

Creating Custom Decorators

Creating custom decorators in Python allows you to add specific functionality to functions or methods in a reusable and modular way. Custom decorators are particularly useful for enhancing behavior, such as logging, timing, or access control, without altering the core logic of the functions they decorate. Here's a guide on how to create and use custom decorators effectively.

Understanding the Basics

A decorator is essentially a function that takes another function (or method) as an argument and returns a new function that usually extends or modifies the original function's behavior.

Basic Syntax of a Decorator
python
Copy code
```
def my_decorator(func):
    def wrapper(*args, **kwargs):
        # Additional behavior before calling the original function
        result = func(*args, **kwargs)
        # Additional behavior after calling the original function
        return result
    return wrapper
```
my_decorator is the custom decorator function.

func is the function being decorated.

wrapper is the inner function that extends or modifies the behavior of func.

Step-by-Step Guide to Creating Custom Decorators

1. Define the Decorator Function

Start by defining a decorator function that takes another function as an argument. Within this function, define an inner function that performs additional actions before or after calling the original function.

Example: Logging Decorator

python
Copy code

```python
def log_function_call(func):
    def wrapper(*args, **kwargs):
        print(f"Calling {func.__name__} with arguments {args} and {kwargs}")
        result = func(*args, **kwargs)
        print(f"{func.__name__} returned {result}")
        return result
    return wrapper
```

In this example, log_function_call logs the function name, arguments, and return value.

2. Apply the Decorator

Use the @decorator_name syntax above the function definition to apply the decorator.

Example:

```python
Copy code
@log_function_call
def add(x, y):
    return x + y
```

add(5, 3)
When add is called, it will now also log the call details due to the log_function_call decorator.

3. Handling Parameters in Decorators

If you need a decorator that accepts parameters, you can create a decorator factory. This is a decorator that returns another decorator.

Example: Repeating Decorator

```python
Copy code
def repeat(times):
    def decorator(func):
```

```python
    def wrapper(*args, **kwargs):
        result = func(*args, **kwargs)
        return [result] * times
    return wrapper
  return decorator
```
Apply the decorator with parameters:

python
Copy code
```python
@repeat(3)
def get_message(message):
    return message


print(get_message("Hello"))   # Output: ['Hello', 'Hello', 'Hello']
```

4. Using functools.wraps

To preserve the metadata (such as the function name and docstring) of the original function, use functools.wraps in your decorator.

Example:

```python
Copy code
from functools import wraps

def log_function_call(func):
    @wraps(func)
    def wrapper(*args, **kwargs):
        print(f"Calling {func.__name__} with arguments {args} and {kwargs}")
        result = func(*args, **kwargs)
        print(f"{func.__name__} returned {result}")
        return result
    return wrapper
```

Using @wraps(func) ensures that wrapper retains the original function's metadata.

Advanced Usage

Custom decorators can also be used in combination with other advanced programming techniques:

Class Methods and Static Methods: Decorators can be applied to class methods and static methods to enhance their behavior in a class context.

Context Managers: Decorators can be used to create context managers for resource management and cleanup.

Asynchronous Decorators: Custom decorators can be designed to work with asynchronous functions, allowing for additional functionality in async code.

Summary

Creating custom decorators in Python allows you to extend and modify the behavior of functions in a modular and reusable way. By defining decorators and applying them with the @ syntax, you can add functionality such as logging, caching, or access control to your functions. Custom decorators enhance code readability, maintainability, and adhere to design principles like the Open/Closed Principle.

APPLYING MONADS AND OTHER FUNCTIONAL CONCEPTS

In functional programming, monads and related concepts offer sophisticated tools for managing complex computations and side effects in a structured and reusable manner. By encapsulating and abstracting operations, these concepts facilitate clean, modular, and maintainable code. Monads help in sequencing actions and managing contexts like optional values or side effects, while other functional concepts like functors and applicatives provide additional mechanisms for handling data transformations and combining computations. Understanding and applying these functional programming principles can lead to more robust and expressive software solutions.

What are Monads?

Monads are a fundamental concept in functional programming that provide a powerful way to handle computations, manage side effects, and structure code in a predictable and reusable manner. They offer a consistent approach to sequencing operations and managing values within a context, making them valuable tools for both simple and complex programming tasks.

Defining Monads

At their core, monads are a design pattern that allows you to encapsulate and manage operations that involve context, such as handling optional values, managing state, or dealing with computations that might fail. Monads consist of three key components:

Type Constructor: This defines the monadic type that wraps values. For instance, the Maybe monad might wrap a value that could be None (representing the absence of a value) or a valid value.

Unit (or Return): This function wraps a value in the monadic context. It takes a plain value and returns it wrapped in the monad. For example, in the Maybe monad, this would wrap a value in a Just or Nothing context.

Bind (or FlatMap): This function chains operations while preserving the monadic context. It takes a monadic value and a function that returns a monadic value, applies the function, and returns a new monadic value. This is key for sequencing computations and managing context.

Monad Laws

Monads adhere to three important laws that ensure they work correctly and consistently:

Left Identity: Applying unit to a value and then binding a function to it is the same as applying the function directly to the value. Formally: unit(x).bind(f) == f(x).

Right Identity: Binding unit to a monadic value should return the original monadic value. Formally: m.bind(unit) == m.

Associativity: Binding a function to the result of binding another function should be the same as binding the composition of the two functions to the monadic value. Formally: m.bind(f).bind(g) == m.bind(x => f(x).bind(g)).

Common Monad Types

Maybe Monad: Represents computations that may fail. It can be Just(value) for successful computations or Nothing for failures.

```python
Copy code
class Maybe:
    def __init__(self, value):
        self.value = value

    def bind(self, func):
        if self.value is None:
            return self
        return func(self.value)

    @staticmethod
    def unit(value):
        return Maybe(value)
```

Either Monad: Encodes operations that might return an error, where Left represents an error and Right represents a successful value.

```python
Copy code
```

```python
class Either:
    def __init__(self, value):
        self.value = value

    def bind(self, func):
        if isinstance(self, Left):
            return self
        return func(self.value)

    @staticmethod
    def unit(value):
        return Right(value)

class Left(Either):
    pass

class Right(Either):
    pass
```

IO Monad: Manages side effects, such as input and output operations, in a pure functional way.

python
Copy code
```python
class IO:
```

```python
def __init__(self, action):
    self.action = action

def bind(self, func):
    return IO(lambda: func(self.action()).action())

@staticmethod
def unit(value):
    return IO(lambda: value)
```

Benefits of Using Monads

Modular Code: Monads promote modularity by allowing operations to be composed and managed in a consistent manner.

Error Handling: They provide a structured way to handle errors and exceptions, improving code robustness.

Side Effect Management: Monads like the IO monad enable handling of side effects in a controlled manner, preserving the purity of functions.

Readable Code: By abstracting complex operations, monads help in writing cleaner and more maintainable code.

Summary

Monads are a powerful abstraction in functional programming that enable structured management of computations and side effects. They provide a consistent way to handle values within a context, facilitate chaining of operations, and enhance code modularity and readability. Understanding and applying monads can significantly improve your approach to managing complex programming tasks and operations.

Using Monads in Python Programming

While Python does not natively support monads, you can implement monadic patterns to enhance the management of computations and side effects in your code. Monads provide a way to structure and chain operations, handle errors, and manage contexts in a predictable and modular fashion. Here's how you can apply monads in Python programming.

Implementing Monads in Python

To use monads in Python, you need to define a monadic type that follows the monadic interface: a type constructor, a unit function, and a bind function. Let's look at some practical examples.

1. Maybe Monad

The Maybe monad represents computations that might fail. It encapsulates a value that could be None, allowing for safe operations without the need for explicit null checks.

```python
Copy code
class Maybe:
    def __init__(self, value):
        self.value = value

    def bind(self, func):
        if self.value is None:
            return self
        return func(self.value)

    @staticmethod
    def unit(value):
        return Maybe(value)

    def __repr__(self):
```

        return f"Maybe({self.value})"
Usage Example:

```python
Copy code
def safe_divide(x, y):
    if y == 0:
        return Maybe(None)
    return Maybe(x / y)
```

result = Maybe.unit(10).bind(lambda x: safe_divide(x, 2)).bind(lambda x: safe_divide(x, 0))
print(result) # Output: Maybe(None)

2. Either Monad

The Either monad can represent operations that might return an error, where Left is used for errors and Right for successful results.

```python
Copy code
class Either:
    def __init__(self, value):
```

```python
        self.value = value

    def bind(self, func):
        if isinstance(self, Left):
            return self
        return func(self.value)

    @staticmethod
    def unit(value):
        return Right(value)

    def __repr__(self):
        return f"Either({self.value})"

class Left(Either):
    def __init__(self, value):
        super().__init__(value)

class Right(Either):
    def __init__(self, value):
        super().__init__(value)
```
Usage Example:

python
Copy code

```python
def divide(x, y):
    if y == 0:
        return Left("Division by zero error")
    return Right(x / y)


result = Either.unit(10).bind(lambda x: divide(x,
2)).bind(lambda x: divide(x, 0))
print(result)  # Output: Left(Division by zero error)
```

3. IO Monad

The IO monad allows you to encapsulate and manage side
effects like input/output operations in a functional manner.

```python
Copy code
class IO:
    def __init__(self, action):
        self.action = action

    def bind(self, func):
        return IO(lambda: func(self.action()).action())

    @staticmethod
```

```python
def unit(value):
    return IO(lambda: value)

def run(self):
    return self.action()
```
Usage Example:

```python
Copy code
def read_input():
    return input("Enter a value: ")

def print_output(value):
    print(f"You entered: {value}")

program = IO(read_input).bind(lambda x: IO(lambda:
print_output(x)))
program.run()
```

Benefits of Using Monads in Python

Error Handling: Monads like Maybe and Either provide structured approaches to handle errors and edge cases gracefully.

State Management: Monads can help manage state and side effects in a predictable manner, maintaining functional purity.

Code Readability: By encapsulating complex operations, monads improve code readability and maintainability.

Composable Functions: Monadic patterns facilitate composing and chaining functions in a clean and modular way.

Summary

Applying monads in Python allows you to manage computations, handle errors, and control side effects more effectively. By defining monadic types like Maybe, Either, and IO, you can structure your code to be more modular and expressive. While Python's syntax does not natively support monads, implementing these patterns can enhance your programming practices and lead to more robust and maintainable code.

PART IV: PROCEDURAL PROGRAMMING EXCELLENCE

CHAPTER 7
Introduction to Procedural Programming

Procedural programming is a paradigm centered around the concept of procedure calls, where the logic of a program is built around procedures or functions. In this approach, programs are structured as a sequence of steps or instructions that manipulate data, allowing for clear, straightforward execution of tasks. Key principles of procedural programming include:

Procedures/Functions: These are reusable blocks of code that perform specific tasks. They help in organizing code, improving readability, and facilitating code reuse.

Sequential Execution: Instructions are executed in a linear sequence, making it easy to follow and debug.

Variable Scope: Variables are used to store data, and their scope can be local to a function or global across the entire program.

Modularity: Code is divided into smaller, manageable pieces, enhancing maintainability and collaboration.

Procedural programming is commonly used in many programming languages and is a foundational concept for understanding more complex programming paradigms.

WHAT IS PROCEDURAL PROGRAMMING

Procedural programming is a programming paradigm that organizes code into a series of procedures or functions, each designed to perform a specific task. It follows a top-down approach, where a program is viewed as a sequence of steps or instructions that the computer executes in order.

Key characteristics of procedural programming include:

Functions/Procedures: The core components are functions or procedures that encapsulate a specific piece of logic or behavior. These can be called multiple times within a program, promoting code reuse.

Sequential Flow: Instructions are executed in a linear, step-by-step manner, which makes the logic of the program easy to follow and debug.

Global and Local Variables: Variables can be defined globally, accessible throughout the program, or locally within a function, controlling their scope and lifespan.

Modularity: By breaking down complex tasks into smaller, manageable functions, procedural programming fosters a modular structure, making programs easier to maintain and extend.

Procedural programming is widely used and forms the foundation of many modern programming languages like C, Python, and JavaScript. It's ideal for tasks that can be clearly divided into a series of procedures or steps, making it a fundamental concept for new programmers to grasp.

Breaking Down Programs into Functions

Breaking down programs into functions is a key practice in procedural programming that enhances code organization, readability, and reusability. Functions are self-contained blocks of code designed to perform specific tasks, and they can be invoked as needed throughout the program. This approach allows complex problems to be tackled by dividing them into smaller, manageable pieces.

Benefits of Using Functions

Modularity: Functions allow you to segment a program into distinct, logical parts. Each function handles a specific task, making the program easier to understand and maintain.

Code Reusability: Once a function is written, it can be reused in different parts of the program or even in different programs, reducing redundancy and effort.

Simplified Debugging: When a program is divided into functions, errors can be isolated and fixed more easily. Debugging becomes more straightforward because each function can be tested independently.

Enhanced Collaboration: In a team setting, functions allow multiple developers to work on different parts of the program simultaneously, improving efficiency and reducing conflicts.

How to Break Down a Program

Identify Tasks: Start by analyzing the problem and identifying the different tasks that need to be performed. Each task should ideally correspond to a function.

Design Functions: Define functions for each task, giving them descriptive names that clearly indicate their purpose. Decide on the inputs (parameters) they need and the output they will produce.

Implement Functions: Write the code for each function, ensuring it accomplishes its specific task efficiently. Keep functions focused and avoid making them too complex or multi-purpose.

Integrate Functions: Combine the functions within the main program, ensuring they work together harmoniously. Functions can call each other to perform more complex operations.

Example
Consider a program that processes a list of numbers to calculate the sum, average, and maximum value. Instead of writing all the logic in one block, you can create separate functions:

```python
Copy code
def calculate_sum(numbers):
    return sum(numbers)

def calculate_average(numbers):
    return sum(numbers) / len(numbers)

def find_maximum(numbers):
    return max(numbers)

numbers = [10, 20, 30, 40, 50]
print("Sum:", calculate_sum(numbers))
print("Average:", calculate_average(numbers))
print("Maximum:", find_maximum(numbers))
```

In this example, each function handles a distinct task, making the code more organized, reusable, and easier to maintain.

Summary

Breaking down programs into functions is a fundamental technique in procedural programming. It enables modularity, enhances code readability and reusability, and simplifies debugging and maintenance. By dividing complex tasks into smaller, focused functions, you create programs that are easier to understand, manage, and extend.

Understanding Control Flow

Control flow refers to the order in which individual statements, instructions, or function calls are executed or evaluated in a program. It's a fundamental concept in programming that dictates how a program proceeds based on various conditions and loops, allowing for decision-making, repetition, and branching within the code.

Types of Control Flow Constructs

Sequential Execution:

The default mode of operation in most programming languages, where statements are executed one after the other in the order they are written.

Conditional Statements:

if Statements: Allow the program to execute certain blocks of code only if a specific condition is true.

else and elif (else if) Statements: Provide alternative paths of execution if the initial if condition is false.

switch/case Statements (in some languages): Offer a way to compare a variable against multiple values and execute the corresponding block of code.

Example in Python:

```python
Copy code
x = 10
if x > 5:
    print("x is greater than 5")
elif x == 5:
    print("x is equal to 5")
else:
    print("x is less than 5")
```

Loops:

for Loops: Execute a block of code repeatedly for a fixed number of times, often iterating over a sequence (like a list or range).

while Loops: Continue to execute a block of code as long as a specific condition remains true.

do-while Loops (in some languages): Similar to while loops, but they execute the block at least once before checking the condition.

Example in Python:

```python
Copy code
for i in range(5):
    print(i)  # Prints numbers 0 to 4

count = 0
while count < 5:
    print(count)
    count += 1  # Prints numbers 0 to 4
```

Control Flow Statements:

break: Exits the loop prematurely, usually when a certain condition is met.

continue: Skips the current iteration of the loop and proceeds to the next iteration.

return: Exits a function and optionally returns a value.

Example in Python:

```python
Copy code
for i in range(10):
    if i == 5:
        break  # Stops the loop when i equals 5
    if i % 2 == 0:
        continue  # Skips even numbers
    print(i)  # Prints odd numbers 1, 3, and stops before 5
```

Function Calls:

Functions encapsulate a block of code that can be executed when called. Control flow can jump to a function when it's called and return to the point of the call after the function completes.

Example in Python:

```python
Copy code
```

```python
def greet(name):
    print(f"Hello, {name}!")

greet("Alice")  # Control flow jumps to the greet function
```

Importance of Control Flow

Decision-Making: Control flow allows programs to make decisions and execute different actions based on different conditions.

Repetition: By using loops, control flow enables the repetition of actions without rewriting code, making programs more concise and efficient.

Organization: Proper use of control flow structures makes the code more readable, maintainable, and scalable.

Summary
Understanding control flow is crucial for writing effective programs. It determines the path your program takes during execution, enabling complex decision-making, repeated actions, and more organized, efficient code. By mastering control flow constructs like conditionals, loops, and

function calls, you can create dynamic and responsive programs that handle a wide variety of tasks and conditions.

WRITING MODULAR CODE

Writing modular code is a best practice in software development that involves breaking down a program into smaller, self-contained units or modules. Each module is designed to handle a specific piece of functionality, making the code more organized, easier to maintain, and reusable. Modular code is essential for creating scalable and robust applications, as it promotes separation of concerns, enhances collaboration among developers, and simplifies debugging and testing.

In modular programming, the focus is on creating functions, classes, or components that encapsulate specific tasks or features. These modules can be independently developed, tested, and reused across different parts of an application or even in other projects. By adhering to the principles of modularity, developers can build complex systems that are easier to understand, modify, and extend over time.

Creating Reusable Functions

Creating reusable functions is a core practice in software development that enhances efficiency, reduces redundancy, and simplifies code maintenance. Reusable functions are designed to perform specific tasks that can be applied across different parts of a program or even in multiple projects. By writing functions that are general enough to handle a variety of inputs and scenarios, you can save time and effort in the long run.

Key Principles of Reusable Functions

Single Responsibility:

Each function should have a single, well-defined purpose. By focusing on one task, the function becomes more predictable, easier to test, and simpler to reuse in different contexts.

Parameterization:

Functions should be designed to accept parameters, allowing them to operate on different data without modification. This flexibility is crucial for making functions applicable to a wide range of situations.

Example:

```python
Copy code
def greet_user(name):
    return f"Hello, {name}!"


print(greet_user("Alice"))  # Outputs: Hello, Alice!
print(greet_user("Bob"))    # Outputs: Hello, Bob!
```

Avoiding Hard-Coded Values:

Instead of embedding specific values within the function, use parameters or configuration options. This approach increases the function's adaptability and reusability.

Return Values:

A reusable function should return a result rather than printing it directly, allowing the calling code to decide how to use the output. This practice makes the function more versatile and easier to integrate into different parts of a program.

Example:

```python
Copy code
def calculate_area(length, width):
    return length * width

area1 = calculate_area(5, 10)  # Returns 50
area2 = calculate_area(3, 7)   # Returns 21
```

Documentation and Naming:

Clear, descriptive names and documentation help others (and your future self) understand what the function does and how to use it. This clarity is essential for promoting reuse and collaboration.

Example:

```python
Copy code
def is_even(number):
    """
    Check if a number is even.

    Args:
        number (int): The number to check.

    Returns:
        bool: True if the number is even, False otherwise.
    """
    return number % 2 == 0
```

Testing and Validation:

To ensure reliability, reusable functions should be thoroughly tested with various inputs, including edge cases. This testing helps guarantee that the function will behave correctly in different scenarios.

Benefits of Reusable Functions

Efficiency: By reusing functions, you avoid duplicating code, reducing the amount of work required to implement similar features.

Consistency: Reusing functions across different parts of a program ensures consistent behavior and reduces the chance of errors.

Maintenance: When a function is updated or improved, all parts of the program that use it benefit from the change, making maintenance easier and more manageable.

Scalability: Reusable functions make it easier to scale and extend applications by building on existing code rather than starting from scratch.

Summary

Creating reusable functions is a powerful technique that promotes code efficiency, consistency, and maintainability. By adhering to principles such as single responsibility, parameterization, and clear documentation, you can develop functions that are adaptable and applicable across various parts of your program or even in different projects. Reusable functions not only streamline the development process but also contribute to the long-term success and scalability of your software.

Organizing Code into Modules and Packages

Organizing code into modules and packages is an essential practice in software development that enhances code structure, maintainability, and scalability. By breaking down your codebase into well-defined modules and grouping related modules into packages, you can manage complexity, improve code reuse, and collaborate more effectively with other developers.

Modules: The Building Blocks

A module is a single file (usually with a .py extension in Python) that contains related functions, classes, or variables. Modules help you encapsulate functionality into separate, manageable units. This separation allows you to focus on specific aspects of your program independently, making it easier to test, debug, and maintain.

Benefits of Using Modules:

Separation of Concerns: Modules allow you to separate different parts of your code based on functionality. For example, you might have one module for handling data processing, another for interacting with a database, and a third for managing user input.

Code Reusability: By placing related functions and classes in a module, you can easily reuse them across different parts of your program or even in other projects.

Namespace Management: Modules help avoid naming conflicts by encapsulating their content in a unique namespace. This means you can use the same function or variable names in different modules without causing clashes.

Simplified Debugging: Smaller, self-contained modules are easier to test and debug, as you can isolate issues more effectively.

Example of a Module:
Imagine you have a file named math_operations.py containing the following code:

python
Copy code

```python
def add(a, b):
    return a + b

def subtract(a, b):
    return a - b

def multiply(a, b):
    return a * b

def divide(a, b):
    if b != 0:
        return a / b
    else:
        return "Cannot divide by zero"
```

This file can be imported as a module in other parts of your program:

python
Copy code
```python
import math_operations as math_ops

result = math_ops.add(10, 5)
print(result)  # Outputs: 15
```

Packages: Grouping Modules Together

A package is a directory that contains multiple related modules. It often includes an __init__.py file, which indicates to Python that the directory should be treated as a package. Packages help you organize larger projects by grouping related modules into a coherent structure.

Benefits of Using Packages:

Organized Structure: Packages allow you to create a hierarchical structure, making it easier to navigate and understand large codebases. For instance, you can have packages for different functionalities like data_processing, user_interface, and database.

Scalability: As your project grows, you can easily add new modules to existing packages or create new packages to handle additional features.

Encapsulation: Packages help encapsulate code into distinct, logical groupings, making it easier to manage dependencies and maintain a clean codebase.

Example of a Package:
Consider a package structure like this:

```markdown
markdown
Copy code
my_project/
    __init__.py
    data_processing/
        __init__.py
        data_cleaning.py
        data_visualization.py
    database/
        __init__.py
        db_connection.py
        db_queries.py
    user_interface/
        __init__.py
        ui_manager.py
        ui_elements.py
```

In this example, each directory (data_processing, database, user_interface) is a package containing related modules. You can import and use these modules in your main program like this:

```python
python
Copy code
from data_processing.data_cleaning import clean_data
```

```
from database.db_connection import connect_to_db

cleaned_data = clean_data(raw_data)
connection = connect_to_db()
```

Summary

Organizing code into modules and packages is a crucial strategy for managing complexity in software projects. Modules provide a way to encapsulate related functionality into self-contained units, while packages help group these modules into organized, scalable structures. By leveraging modules and packages, you can create more maintainable, reusable, and understandable code, making your development process smoother and more efficient.

CHAPTER 8

Advanced Procedural Programming

Advanced procedural programming builds upon the fundamental concepts of procedural programming, focusing on more sophisticated techniques to enhance code efficiency, readability, and maintainability. While basic procedural programming involves breaking down tasks into functions and controlling the flow of the program using conditionals and loops, advanced techniques push these principles further by emphasizing modularity, code reuse, and performance optimization.

In advanced procedural programming, you delve into areas such as algorithm optimization, advanced function usage (including recursion and higher-order functions), and modular code organization. These techniques allow you to write more complex, efficient, and scalable programs. Additionally, advanced error handling, data manipulation, and memory management techniques are explored to ensure that your code is robust and reliable, even in demanding or unexpected conditions.

By mastering advanced procedural programming, you can create more sophisticated and performant software that can handle a wider range of tasks while maintaining clarity and maintainability. This foundation also sets the stage for integrating with other paradigms, such as object-oriented or functional programming, allowing you to choose the best approach for each part of your application.

OPTIMIZING ALGORITHMS FOR PERFORMANCE

Optimizing algorithms for performance is a critical aspect of advanced programming that focuses on improving the efficiency of your code to handle larger datasets, execute faster, and use fewer resources. As programs grow in complexity and scale, the performance of algorithms becomes increasingly important, especially in environments where time and resource constraints are significant.

In this context, optimization involves analyzing the time and space complexity of algorithms, selecting the most appropriate data structures, and applying advanced techniques like memoization, dynamic programming, and parallel processing. These strategies help reduce the computational load, minimize memory usage, and enhance the overall responsiveness of your software.

By learning how to optimize algorithms, you not only improve the performance of your current programs but also develop the skills to design future applications that are scalable and efficient from the ground up. This process is essential in fields such as data science, machine learning, and systems programming, where the ability to process large volumes of data quickly and efficiently is paramount.

Efficient Sorting and Searching Techniques

Efficient sorting and searching techniques are fundamental to optimizing the performance of algorithms and data processing tasks. These techniques are crucial for managing and retrieving data quickly, especially when dealing with large datasets or performance-critical applications.

Sorting Techniques

Sorting is the process of arranging data in a specific order, typically ascending or descending. Efficient sorting algorithms are designed to minimize the time complexity of the sorting process.

Quick Sort:

Overview: Quick Sort is a divide-and-conquer algorithm that works by selecting a 'pivot' element and partitioning the array into two sub-arrays—elements less than the pivot and elements greater than the pivot. It recursively sorts the sub-arrays.

Complexity: Average case time complexity is

O

$($

n

$\log$

l

n

$)$

O(nlogn), but the worst case is

O

$($

n

2

$)$

O(n

2

) (though this can be mitigated with good pivot selection strategies).

Merge Sort:

Overview: Merge Sort divides the array into smaller sub-arrays, sorts each sub-array, and then merges them to produce a sorted array. It is known for its stability and predictable performance.

Complexity: Time complexity is

O

$($

n

$\log$

n

$)$

O(nlogn) in all cases, making it efficient and reliable for large datasets.

Heap Sort:

Overview: Heap Sort builds a binary heap from the data and repeatedly extracts the maximum (or minimum) element to build the sorted array. It's an in-place sorting algorithm.

Complexity: Time complexity is

O

$($

n

$\log$

n

$)$

O(nlogn), and it has a constant space complexity of

O

$($

1

$)$

O(1) beyond the input array.

Radix Sort:

Overview: Radix Sort processes numbers digit by digit, starting from the least significant digit to the most significant. It uses a stable sorting algorithm as a subroutine (often counting sort) to sort digits.

Complexity: Time complexity is

O

$($

n

$\cdot$

k

$)$

O(n·k), where

k

k is the number of digits in the maximum number. It is effective for sorting integers or fixed-size records.

Searching Techniques
Searching algorithms are used to find specific elements within a dataset. Efficient searching is vital for applications where quick data retrieval is needed.

Binary Search:

Overview: Binary Search works on sorted arrays by repeatedly dividing the search interval in half. It compares the target value with the middle element and discards half of the search space based on the comparison.
Complexity: Time complexity is

$O(\log n)$
O(logn), making it very efficient for large sorted datasets.

Linear Search:

Overview: Linear Search scans each element in the array sequentially until the target element is found or the end of the array is reached.

Complexity: Time complexity is

O

$($

n

$)$

O(n). It is simple and effective for small or unsorted datasets but less efficient for larger, sorted datasets compared to Binary Search.

Hashing:

Overview: Hashing involves mapping data to a fixed-size hash table using a hash function. It allows for average-case constant time complexity for search, insert, and delete operations.

Complexity: Time complexity is

O

$($

1

$)$

O(1) on average, though it can degrade to

O

(

n

)

O(n) in cases of hash collisions.

Interpolation Search:

Overview: Interpolation Search improves upon Binary Search by estimating the position of the target value based on the value's relative position within the sorted array.

Complexity: Time complexity is

O

(

log

log

n

)

O(loglogn) for uniformly distributed data but

O

(

n

)

$O(n)$ in the worst case.

Summary

Efficient sorting and searching techniques are essential for handling data effectively and optimizing program performance. By choosing the appropriate algorithm based on the dataset characteristics and requirements, you can significantly improve the speed and efficiency of your applications. Understanding and applying these techniques is crucial for developing scalable and high-performance software solutions.

Complexity Analysis and Optimization

Complexity analysis and optimization are fundamental practices in computer science aimed at improving the efficiency and performance of algorithms. Understanding how to analyze and optimize code helps in building software that scales well with increasing input sizes and performs efficiently under varying conditions.

Complexity Analysis

Complexity analysis involves evaluating an algorithm's efficiency in terms of time and space resources. It provides insights into how an algorithm's performance grows relative to the input size, allowing developers to make informed decisions about which algorithms to use.

Time Complexity:

Definition: Time complexity measures the amount of time an algorithm takes to complete as a function of the input size. It is expressed using Big O notation (e.g.,

O

$($

n

$)$

O(n),

O

$($

log

n

)
$O(\log n)$,

O

$($

n

2

$)$

$O(n$

2

$))$.

Purpose: Helps in understanding how the execution time increases with larger inputs, allowing for the selection of more efficient algorithms for time-critical applications.

Example:

A linear search algorithm has a time complexity of

O

$($

n

$)$

$O(n)$, where

n

n is the number of elements in the dataset. This means that the time required to search increases linearly with the size of the dataset.

Space Complexity:

Definition: Space complexity measures the amount of memory an algorithm uses relative to the input size. It is also expressed using Big O notation.

Purpose: Helps in understanding how the memory requirements of an algorithm scale, which is crucial for memory-limited environments.

Example:

A recursive algorithm with

$$O$$

$$($$

$$n$$

$$)$$

O(n) space complexity uses additional memory proportional to the depth of recursion.

Best, Average, and Worst-Case Complexity:

Best Case: The scenario where the algorithm performs the minimum number of operations.

Average Case: The expected performance over a distribution of inputs.

Worst Case: The scenario where the algorithm performs the maximum number of operations.

Example:

Quick Sort has an average time complexity of

O

$($

n

$\log$

n

$)$

O(nlogn) but can degrade to

O

$($

n

2

$)$

O(n

2

) in the worst case if the pivot selection is poor.

Optimization Techniques

Optimization involves improving an algorithm or code to enhance its performance or resource usage. It focuses on reducing time complexity, space complexity, or both, to achieve more efficient execution.

Algorithm Optimization:

Selecting the Right Algorithm: Choosing the most appropriate algorithm based on time and space complexity for the problem at hand.

Improving Algorithms: Refining algorithms to reduce their time complexity or enhance their performance. Techniques include dynamic programming, memoization, and optimization heuristics.

Example:

Replacing a naive
O

$($

n

2

$)$

$O(n$

2

$)$ sorting algorithm with Merge Sort or Quick Sort, both of which have better average-case performance.

Code Optimization:

Profiling: Analyzing code performance using profiling tools to identify bottlenecks and inefficient code sections.

Refactoring: Improving the code structure and efficiency without changing its functionality. This includes eliminating redundant calculations and optimizing loops and recursive calls.

Parallelism and Concurrency: Utilizing multiple processors or cores to perform tasks simultaneously, which can significantly speed up computation.

Example:

Parallelizing tasks that can be executed independently, such as processing large datasets using multi-threading or distributed computing.

Memory Optimization:

Efficient Data Structures: Using data structures that provide efficient access and manipulation, such as hash tables for quick lookups or heaps for priority queues.
Memory Management: Reducing memory footprint by minimizing the use of large data structures and avoiding memory leaks.

Example:

Using an array instead of a linked list when frequent access by index is required, as arrays provide constant time access compared to linear time for linked lists.

Summary
Complexity analysis and optimization are essential for developing efficient algorithms and software. By understanding the time and space complexity of algorithms and applying optimization techniques, you can ensure that

your programs perform well, even with large datasets or under heavy load conditions. Effective complexity analysis and optimization not only enhance performance but also contribute to the scalability and robustness of software applications.

UTILIZING MULTI-THREADING AND CONCURRENCY

Utilizing multi-threading and concurrency is crucial for enhancing the performance and responsiveness of modern applications, especially those requiring simultaneous execution of tasks. These concepts enable programs to handle multiple operations concurrently, improving efficiency and responsiveness by leveraging the capabilities of multi-core processors and asynchronous processing.

Multi-Threading

Multi-threading involves dividing a program into multiple threads that can run simultaneously. Each thread operates independently but shares the same resources, such as memory, with other threads within the same process. This approach is particularly useful for tasks that can be performed in parallel, such as background computations, I/O operations, or handling multiple user requests.

Benefits:

Improved Responsiveness: Multi-threading allows applications to remain responsive by performing time-consuming operations in the background, preventing the main thread from becoming unresponsive.
Enhanced Utilization of Multi-Core Processors: By running multiple threads simultaneously, applications can take full advantage of multi-core processors, leading to better performance.

Challenges:

Concurrency Issues: Threads may interfere with each other, leading to issues such as race conditions or deadlocks. Proper synchronization mechanisms are required to manage access to shared resources.
Complex Debugging: Multi-threaded programs can be more challenging to debug due to the non-deterministic nature of thread execution.
Concurrency

Concurrency is a broader concept that encompasses various techniques for executing multiple tasks at the same time, not necessarily involving multiple threads. It includes multi-threading, but also other models such as asynchronous programming, parallelism, and distributed computing.

Benefits:

Efficient Resource Utilization: Concurrency allows different parts of a program to operate simultaneously, leading to better resource utilization and reduced waiting times.
Improved Scalability: Concurrency enables applications to handle a larger number of tasks or users concurrently, enhancing scalability.

.Techniques:

Asynchronous Programming: Involves writing code that performs tasks asynchronously, allowing other tasks to continue running while waiting for long-running operations to complete. This is often achieved using callbacks, promises, or async/await constructs.
Parallelism: Refers to the simultaneous execution of multiple tasks or processes, often on different processors or

cores. It involves breaking down a task into smaller sub-tasks that can be processed concurrently.

Summary

Utilizing multi-threading and concurrency is essential for developing high-performance, responsive applications that can efficiently handle multiple tasks simultaneously. By leveraging these techniques, you can enhance the performance and scalability of your programs, make better use of system resources, and improve user experience. However, it is important to be aware of the challenges associated with concurrency and multi-threading, such as synchronization issues and complex debugging, to effectively manage and optimize concurrent operations in your software.

Understanding Python's GIL

Python's Global Interpreter Lock (GIL) is a mechanism used in the CPython interpreter (the standard implementation of Python) to ensure that only one thread executes Python bytecode at a time. This lock is crucial for maintaining thread safety in the interpreter, particularly in the context of Python's memory management and garbage collection.

What is the GIL?

The GIL is a mutex that protects access to Python objects, preventing multiple native threads from executing Python bytecodes simultaneously. Its primary purpose is to simplify the implementation of CPython's memory management and ensure that Python objects are not corrupted by concurrent modifications.

Implications of the GIL

Single Thread Execution:

Concurrency Limitations: The GIL can limit the effectiveness of multi-threading in CPU-bound tasks, where multiple threads are competing for CPU time. Because only one thread can execute Python code at a time, true parallel execution of Python bytecode is not possible within a single process.

I/O-Bound Tasks: For I/O-bound operations (such as file or network operations), the GIL is less of a bottleneck. Threads waiting for I/O operations to complete can release the GIL, allowing other threads to run.

Performance Considerations:

CPU-Bound Programs: In CPU-bound programs, where threads are performing computations, the GIL can become a performance bottleneck, as it prevents multiple threads from fully utilizing multi-core processors.

Multi-Core Systems: On multi-core systems, the GIL means that multi-threaded Python programs may not see significant performance improvements for CPU-bound tasks compared to single-threaded programs.

.

Workarounds and Alternatives:

Multiprocessing: For CPU-bound tasks, the multiprocessing module is often used as an alternative to multi-threading. It creates separate processes, each with its own Python interpreter and GIL, allowing true parallel execution.

External Libraries: Libraries such as NumPy or other C extensions can release the GIL during computationally intensive operations, allowing them to run in parallel while bypassing the limitations of the GIL.

Managing the GIL

Understanding Context: It's important to understand when the GIL will impact your application. For many I/O-bound applications, the GIL will not be a significant issue, while for CPU-bound applications, considering alternative approaches like multiprocessing or optimizing critical sections of code in C extensions can be beneficial.

Using Python Implementations: Other implementations of Python, such as Jython (Python on the JVM) or IronPython (Python on the .NET framework), do not use the GIL and thus do not have the same limitations, although they may not fully support CPython extensions.

Summary

The Global Interpreter Lock (GIL) is a key feature of CPython that affects how multi-threading works in Python, particularly for CPU-bound tasks. While it simplifies the implementation of thread safety in the interpreter, it can limit the performance of multi-threaded programs on multi-core systems. Understanding the implications of the GIL and exploring alternative strategies such as multiprocessing or external libraries can help mitigate its impact and optimize performance in Python applications.

.

Implementing Concurrency with Threads and Asyncio

Concurrency is a crucial aspect of modern programming, enabling applications to perform multiple tasks simultaneously and efficiently handle tasks that would otherwise cause delays or resource contention. In Python, two prominent approaches for implementing concurrency are threading and asynchronous programming with asyncio. Each has its own use cases and benefits, making it important to understand when and how to use them effectively.

Concurrency with Threads

Threading involves running multiple threads within the same process, allowing for concurrent execution of tasks. Threads share the same memory space but operate independently, which can be beneficial for tasks that require parallel execution.

Using the threading Module:

Basic Usage: The threading module provides a way to create and manage threads. You can define a thread by subclassing threading.Thread or by passing a function to threading.Thread and then calling the start() method to initiate the thread.

Example:
python
Copy code
```python
import threading

def print_numbers():
    for i in range(10):
        print(i)

def print_letters():
    for letter in 'abcdefghij':
```

```
    print(letter)

thread1 = threading.Thread(target=print_numbers)
thread2 = threading.Thread(target=print_letters)

thread1.start()
thread2.start()

thread1.join()
thread2.join()
```

Advantages:

Simplicity: Threading is relatively straightforward for tasks that can be parallelized, such as handling multiple I/O operations.
Shared Resources: Threads share the same memory space, which can make communication between threads easier compared to processes.

.

.Limitations:

GIL Impact: Due to Python's Global Interpreter Lock (GIL), threading does not provide true parallel execution for CPU-bound tasks in CPython. The GIL limits the ability to fully utilize multi-core processors for Python bytecode execution.

Synchronization Issues: Threads require careful management to avoid issues such as race conditions and deadlocks.

Concurrency with Asyncio

asyncio is a library in Python designed for writing asynchronous code using the async/await syntax. It is particularly effective for I/O-bound tasks and can be used to handle thousands of concurrent operations without the overhead of threading.

Using asyncio:

Async Functions: Define asynchronous functions using the async def keyword, and use the await keyword to call other asynchronous functions.

Event Loop: The asyncio event loop manages the execution of asynchronous tasks, scheduling them and handling their completion.

Example:
python

```
Copy code
import asyncio

async def fetch_data():
    print('Fetching data...')
    await asyncio.sleep(2)
    print('Data fetched')

async def main():
    await asyncio.gather(fetch_data(), fetch_data())

asyncio.run(main())
```
.

Advantages:

Efficiency: asyncio is designed for high concurrency with low overhead, making it ideal for I/O-bound and network-bound tasks.

Scalability: It can handle many concurrent operations using a single thread, which can be more resource-efficient than threading or multiprocessing.

.Limitations:

Complexity: Asynchronous programming can be more complex to reason about compared to synchronous code, particularly when dealing with multiple layers of asynchronous calls.

Not for CPU-Bound Tasks: While asyncio is effective for I/O-bound tasks, it is not suitable for CPU-bound operations that require parallel execution.

Choosing Between Threads and Asyncio

Use Threads When:

You need to perform parallel tasks that are mostly I/O-bound or that involve blocking operations.
You are working with existing synchronous code that needs to be parallelized without a complete rewrite.

Use Asyncio When:

You are working with I/O-bound tasks that involve a lot of waiting (e.g., network requests, file I/O) and you want to achieve high concurrency with minimal resource usage.

You are developing applications that can benefit from non-blocking operations and need to handle many concurrent tasks efficiently.

Summary

Implementing concurrency with threads and asyncio provides different approaches for managing multiple tasks simultaneously in Python. Threads are useful for parallelizing tasks in a straightforward manner, though they may be limited by the GIL for CPU-bound tasks. Asyncio offers a powerful alternative for handling high levels of concurrency with I/O-bound tasks, enabling efficient asynchronous programming with low overhead. Choosing the right approach depends on the nature of the tasks and the specific requirements of your application.

PART V: COMBINING PARADIGMS FOR ROBUST APPLICATIONS

CHAPTER 9
Hybrid Programming Approaches

In the dynamic world of software development, a one-size-fits-all approach often falls short when addressing complex and varied programming challenges. Hybrid programming approaches provide a powerful solution by combining multiple paradigms—such as object-oriented, functional, and procedural programming—and integrating different concurrency models like threading and asynchronous programming. This blend allows developers to harness the unique strengths of each method, creating more efficient, adaptable, and scalable software solutions.

Why Opt for Hybrid Approaches?
Versatility: Different programming paradigms are suited to different types of tasks. By blending these paradigms, you can tackle a wider range of problems more effectively, using the most appropriate tools for each aspect of your application.

Optimized Performance: Hybrid approaches enable the use of various concurrency techniques, such as combining multi-threading with asynchronous programming, to maximize resource utilization and improve the performance of both CPU-bound and I/O-bound tasks.

Modular and Maintainable Code: Mixing paradigms can lead to better-organized code, where each component is developed using the paradigm that best suits its role. This results in a cleaner, more maintainable codebase that is easier to understand and extend.

Challenges and Considerations
While hybrid programming offers many benefits, it also introduces complexity. Integrating different paradigms requires careful planning to ensure compatibility and prevent conflicts, such as managing mutable state across different programming models or avoiding concurrency pitfalls when combining threading and async operations.

Conclusion
Hybrid programming approaches in Python offer a strategic way to address the diverse demands of modern software development. By blending paradigms and techniques, developers can create robust, flexible, and high-performance

applications that are well-suited to handle a variety of challenges. Understanding how to effectively combine these methods is key to unlocking their full potential in your projects.

WHEN TO MIX PARADIGMS

In software development, no single programming paradigm perfectly addresses every challenge. That's where mixing paradigms becomes a powerful strategy. Combining different programming styles—such as object-oriented, functional, and procedural programming—allows developers to leverage the strengths of each paradigm, creating more versatile and robust solutions.

Why Consider Mixing Paradigms?
Complexity Management: Some problems are multifaceted, requiring the organizational benefits of object-oriented programming (OOP) alongside the simplicity and power of

functional programming (FP) for specific tasks like data manipulation.

Performance Optimization: Certain paradigms excel in different areas of performance. For instance, OOP is well-suited for managing complex data structures, while FP can be more efficient for tasks involving data transformations. By combining these approaches, you can optimize both the clarity and speed of your code.

Maintainability and Scalability: Mixing paradigms can help create a codebase that is easier to maintain and scale. For example, you might use procedural code for straightforward tasks, OOP for managing state and behavior, and FP for concise, stateless operations.

When to Mix?
When Dealing with Diverse Requirements: If your application requires handling various types of tasks, mixing paradigms can provide the flexibility needed to meet different needs effectively.

When Optimizing for Specific Goals: If certain parts of your codebase would benefit from a different approach—such as using FP to reduce side effects in a primarily OOP system—mixing paradigms can help achieve these goals.

When Enhancing Code Readability: Sometimes, the best way to make code more understandable is to use the paradigm that naturally fits the problem, even if it means combining different styles within the same project.

Conclusion

Mixing paradigms is a sophisticated approach that allows developers to tailor their code to the specific needs of their applications. By carefully choosing when and how to combine different programming styles, you can create software that is not only efficient and powerful but also easier to maintain and extend. Understanding when to mix paradigms is key to mastering this versatile programming strategy.

Combining Object-Oriented and Functional Styles

Combining object-oriented programming (OOP) and functional programming (FP) allows developers to harness the strengths of both paradigms, resulting in code that is both modular and expressive. This hybrid approach is particularly useful in Python, which supports multiple paradigms, giving developers the flexibility to blend OOP's encapsulation with FP's concise, stateless functions.

The Strengths of Each Paradigm

Object-Oriented Programming (OOP):

Encapsulation: OOP excels at organizing complex systems by encapsulating data and behavior into objects. This makes it easier to model real-world entities and manage state.
Inheritance and Polymorphism: These features allow for code reuse and the creation of flexible and scalable systems.
Modularity: Classes and objects help in breaking down large systems into smaller, manageable pieces, promoting maintainability.
Functional Programming (FP):

Immutability: FP emphasizes the use of immutable data, reducing the likelihood of bugs related to shared state and making code easier to reason about.

Higher-Order Functions: Functions can be passed as arguments, returned from other functions, and stored in data structures, leading to more flexible and reusable code.

Conciseness: FP encourages writing short, expressive functions that perform specific tasks, often leading to clearer and more maintainable code.

Benefits of Combining OOP and FP

Improved Code Reusability: By integrating functional techniques like higher-order functions or pure functions within an OOP framework, you can create components that are highly reusable. For instance, you can define a class with methods that accept functions as arguments, allowing you to customize behavior without altering the class itself.

Enhanced Modularity: While OOP provides a natural way to group related data and behavior, FP helps break down logic into small, testable units. This combination can lead to a more modular and testable codebase.

Simplified State Management: OOP typically involves managing state within objects, which can lead to complex dependencies. Incorporating FP concepts like immutability and stateless functions can simplify state management, making your code more predictable and less prone to errors.

Greater Flexibility: Combining paradigms allows you to choose the best approach for each specific problem. For example, you might use FP for data processing within an OOP framework, allowing for cleaner, more efficient code.

Examples of Hybrid Code
Using Functional Methods in OOP:

python
Copy code
```
class DataProcessor:
    def __init__(self, data):
        self.data = data

    def filter_data(self, filter_func):
        return list(filter(filter_func, self.data))

    def transform_data(self, transform_func):
        return list(map(transform_func, self.data))

# Example usage
```

```
processor = DataProcessor([1, 2, 3, 4, 5])
filtered = processor.filter_data(lambda x: x % 2 == 0)
transformed = processor.transform_data(lambda x: x ** 2)
```

Applying Higher-Order Functions in OOP:

python
Copy code

```python
class Calculator:
    def __init__(self, operation):
        self.operation = operation

    def compute(self, x, y):
        return self.operation(x, y)

# Example usage
adder = Calculator(lambda x, y: x + y)
result = adder.compute(5, 3)  # Output: 8
```

Challenges and Considerations

Balancing Complexity: While combining paradigms offers many advantages, it can also introduce complexity. Developers must be cautious not to overcomplicate the codebase by mixing paradigms inappropriately.

Maintaining Consistency: It's important to maintain consistency in how and where you apply each paradigm. Establishing clear guidelines on when to use OOP versus FP can help in maintaining a clean and understandable codebase.

Conclusion

Combining object-oriented and functional programming styles in Python enables you to build software that is both powerful and maintainable. By leveraging the encapsulation and modularity of OOP alongside the expressiveness and simplicity of FP, you can create code that is easier to reason about, test, and extend. This hybrid approach allows you to address the unique challenges of your project with the most effective tools available.

Balancing Procedural and Functional Elements

Balancing procedural and functional programming elements involves integrating the structured, step-by-step approach of procedural programming with the declarative, stateless principles of functional programming. This hybrid approach allows developers to leverage the strengths of both paradigms, creating code that is both efficient and maintainable.

Strengths of Each Paradigm

Procedural Programming:

Sequential Logic: Procedural programming is centered around the execution of a sequence of instructions. It excels in scenarios where tasks can be broken down into clear, linear steps.

Simple State Management: By organizing code into procedures or functions, procedural programming makes it straightforward to manage and understand the flow of data and control.
Ease of Learning: Its structured approach is often easier for beginners to grasp, making it a good starting point for new developers.

Functional Programming:

Immutability and Side-Effect Freedom: Functional programming emphasizes the use of immutable data and pure functions, which do not alter external state. This can lead to more predictable and bug-resistant code.

Higher-Order Functions: FP supports the use of functions as first-class citizens, allowing functions to be passed as arguments, returned as results, and stored in data structures. This enhances code reusability and flexibility.

Declarative Approach: FP focuses on what should be done rather than how it should be done, often leading to more concise and readable code.

Benefits of Combining Procedural and Functional Elements Enhanced Code Clarity: Combining the clear, step-by-step instructions of procedural programming with the declarative nature of functional programming can lead to code that is both easy to follow and expressive. For example, procedural functions can handle complex workflows, while functional techniques can simplify data manipulation.

Improved Maintainability: Functional programming principles, such as immutability and stateless functions, can help manage state more cleanly within a procedural codebase. This can reduce bugs and make the code easier to understand and maintain.

Flexibility in Problem Solving: By leveraging procedural techniques for task sequencing and functional methods for data transformation, you can address a wide range of programming challenges more effectively. This hybrid approach provides flexibility in choosing the right tool for each part of your application.

Examples of Hybrid Code
Using Functional Techniques in Procedural Code:

python
Copy code
```python
# Procedural code with functional techniques
def process_data(data):
    # Using a functional approach to filter and transform data
    filtered_data = list(filter(lambda x: x > 0, data))
    transformed_data = list(map(lambda x: x * 2, filtered_data))
    return transformed_data

data = [1, -2, 3, -4, 5]
result = process_data(data)  # Output: [2, 6, 10]
```
Combining Procedural Flow with Functional Style:

python

Copy code

```
# Procedural flow with functional elements
def calculate_total(values, tax_rate):
    total = sum(values) # Procedural calculation
    tax = total * tax_rate
    return total + tax

values = [100, 200, 300]
total_amount = calculate_total(values, 0.1)   # Output: 660.0
```

Challenges and Considerations

Balancing Complexity: While combining procedural and functional elements can be powerful, it may also introduce complexity. Developers should ensure that the code remains readable and maintainable, avoiding overly intricate hybrids. Consistency: Maintaining a clear approach to when and how each paradigm is used is essential for coherence. Establishing guidelines on integrating procedural and functional elements can help in managing complexity.

Conclusion

Balancing procedural and functional elements allows developers to take advantage of the strengths of both paradigms. Procedural programming offers a straightforward approach to organizing tasks and managing state, while functional programming enhances code clarity and robustness with its emphasis on immutability and higher-order functions. By integrating these elements thoughtfully, you can create code that is both effective and maintainable, addressing a broad range of programming needs.

CASE STUDIES IN MULTI-PARADIGM DESIGN

Case studies in multi-paradigm design provide real-world examples of how integrating various programming paradigms can solve complex challenges and create robust, efficient software solutions. By examining practical applications where different paradigms—such as object-oriented, functional, and procedural programming—are combined, developers can gain insights into effective strategies for leveraging the strengths of each approach.

Why Study Multi-Paradigm Design?

Practical Insights: Case studies offer concrete examples of how combining paradigms can address specific problems, providing valuable lessons and strategies that can be applied to similar challenges in your own projects.

Real-World Applications: Understanding how multi-paradigm design is implemented in real-world scenarios helps bridge the gap between theoretical knowledge and practical application. This can enhance your ability to design and implement effective solutions in your own work.

Innovative Solutions: Case studies often highlight innovative uses of multiple paradigms, showcasing creative approaches to problem-solving and illustrating how diverse programming techniques can be integrated to achieve exceptional results.

What to Expect from Case Studies

Detailed Analysis: Each case study typically includes a detailed examination of the problem, the chosen paradigms, and the implementation approach. This analysis helps in understanding why specific paradigms were selected and how they were combined.

Challenges and Solutions: Case studies often address the challenges encountered during development and how multi-paradigm approaches helped overcome these issues. This can provide practical insights into managing complexity and ensuring effective integration.

Outcome Evaluation: Evaluating the outcomes of multi-paradigm designs helps in assessing the effectiveness of the approach, including performance improvements, maintainability, and overall project success.

Conclusion
Exploring case studies in multi-paradigm design is a valuable way to understand how combining different programming paradigms can be applied to solve real-world problems. These examples offer practical insights and innovative

strategies, helping developers enhance their skills and apply multi-paradigm approaches effectively in their own projects.

Real-World Applications and Their Paradigm Choices

In real-world software development, selecting the appropriate programming paradigm—or combination of paradigms—can significantly impact the efficiency, maintainability, and scalability of applications. Understanding how different paradigms are applied in various domains provides valuable insights into their practical benefits and limitations.

1. Web Development

Paradigms Used: Object-Oriented Programming (OOP), Functional Programming (FP), and Procedural Programming.

Examples:
Django (Python): Uses OOP extensively to model data through classes and manage application state, while also

integrating functional programming elements for data processing and utility functions.

React (JavaScript): Incorporates functional programming principles, such as hooks and stateless components, within a predominantly object-oriented architecture to manage UI state and behavior.

2. Data Science and Machine Learning

Paradigms Used: Functional Programming, Procedural Programming.
Examples:

Pandas (Python): Utilizes functional programming techniques for data transformation and manipulation, applying methods like map, filter, and apply to handle large datasets efficiently.

TensorFlow (Python): Combines procedural code for defining model architectures with functional programming for performing operations on tensors, allowing for flexible and powerful machine learning workflows.

3. Systems Programming

Paradigms Used: Procedural Programming, Functional Programming.

Examples:

Operating Systems (e.g., Linux): Primarily uses procedural programming for implementing system-level functionalities and managing hardware interactions, with functional programming elements for certain high-level abstractions and utilities.

Rust: Employs a mix of procedural and functional programming approaches to achieve memory safety and concurrency, leveraging Rust's strong type system and functional features to manage low-level operations safely and efficiently.

4. Game Development

Paradigms Used: Object-Oriented Programming, Component-Based Design (a variant of OOP), Functional Programming.

Examples:

Unity (C#): Uses object-oriented programming to manage game objects and their behaviors, while functional programming concepts are used for data processing and event handling.

Unreal Engine (C++): Relies on OOP for game object management and functional programming for scripting and event-driven systems, integrating these paradigms to support complex game logic and interactions.

5. Enterprise Applications

Paradigms Used: Object-Oriented Programming, Procedural Programming, Functional Programming.

Examples:

Java Enterprise Edition (Java): Utilizes OOP for modeling business entities and managing application state, procedural programming for application workflows, and increasingly incorporates functional programming features like lambdas and streams for data processing.

Spring Framework (Java): Combines OOP for defining application components and functional programming for reactive programming and handling asynchronous operations.

Conclusion

Real-world applications often require a blend of programming paradigms to address their diverse needs effectively. By understanding how paradigms are applied across different domains, developers can make informed decisions about which approaches to use, leading to more efficient, maintainable, and scalable software solutions. This practical knowledge helps in designing applications that leverage the best aspects of each paradigm, optimizing performance and functionality.

Refactoring Code for Multi-Paradigm Support

Refactoring code to support multiple programming paradigms involves modifying existing codebases to integrate different paradigms effectively. This approach can enhance code readability, maintainability, and performance by leveraging the strengths of each paradigm. Here's how to approach refactoring for multi-paradigm support:

1. Assessing the Current Codebase

Identify Paradigm Gaps: Review the existing codebase to determine which paradigms are currently used and where there might be opportunities to integrate additional paradigms. For instance, a codebase primarily using procedural programming might benefit from incorporating functional programming elements for data processing.

Evaluate Code Complexity: Examine the complexity of the code and identify areas where refactoring could simplify the structure or improve performance. Look for repetitive code, tightly coupled components, or inefficient data handling.

2. Introducing Object-Oriented Programming

Encapsulate Data and Behavior: Refactor procedural code by encapsulating related data and functions into classes. This transformation allows for better organization and reuse of code.

Example: Convert standalone functions into methods of classes and define attributes to manage state.

Implement Inheritance and Polymorphism: Utilize inheritance to create hierarchical class structures and polymorphism to enable flexible method overriding and implementation.

Example: Create base classes for common functionality and derive specialized classes to extend or modify behavior.

3. Integrating Functional Programming Techniques

Refactor to Use Pure Functions: Replace mutable state and side-effects with pure functions that return consistent outputs for given inputs, making code more predictable and testable.

Example: Transform functions that alter global state into functions that operate on passed parameters and return results.

Leverage Higher-Order Functions: Incorporate higher-order functions like map, filter, and reduce to handle data transformations and aggregations more concisely.

Example: Replace loops with map and filter operations to process collections.

4. Adopting Procedural Programming Approaches

Organize Code into Functions: For complex workflows, break down code into well-defined functions that manage specific tasks, promoting code reuse and clarity.

Example: Modularize large code blocks into smaller, focused functions that handle discrete parts of the process.
Improve Control Flow Management: Use procedural programming techniques to manage the flow of execution in a clear and straightforward manner.

Example: Utilize conditional statements and loops to control program flow effectively.

5. Ensuring Seamless Integration
Refactor Gradually: Implement changes incrementally to avoid disrupting existing functionality. Ensure that each refactoring step is tested thoroughly to maintain code stability.

Example: Start by refactoring a single module or function and progressively apply changes to other parts of the codebase.

Maintain Code Readability: While refactoring, prioritize code readability and maintainability. Use clear naming conventions, comments, and documentation to make the codebase easier to understand and manage.

Example: Add comments explaining the purpose of newly introduced paradigms and how they interact with existing code.

6. Testing and Validation

Perform Unit Testing: Develop comprehensive tests to verify that refactored code behaves as expected and does not introduce new bugs. Use unit tests to check the functionality of individual components.

Example: Write test cases for each refactored function or class to ensure correctness.
Conduct Integration Testing: Test the integrated system to ensure that different paradigms work together seamlessly and that overall functionality is preserved.

Example: Validate that interactions between object-oriented, functional, and procedural components operate correctly in the application.

Conclusion

Refactoring code for multi-paradigm support involves systematically incorporating and integrating different programming paradigms to enhance the codebase. By carefully assessing the current code, introducing new paradigms, and ensuring seamless integration, developers can create more efficient, maintainable, and robust software solutions. This approach not only improves code quality but also leverages the strengths of each paradigm to address diverse programming challenges effectively.

CHAPTER 10
Building a Complete Multi-Paradigm Application

Building a complete multi-paradigm application involves integrating various programming paradigms—such as object-oriented, functional, and procedural programming—to create a robust and flexible software solution. This approach allows developers to leverage the strengths of each paradigm, addressing different aspects of the application's needs and enhancing its overall effectiveness.

Why Build Multi-Paradigm Applications?

Enhanced Flexibility: Combining paradigms allows developers to use the best approach for each part of the application. For example, functional programming can be used for data processing, while object-oriented programming can manage complex data structures and relationships.

Improved Maintainability: By applying different paradigms where they fit best, the codebase can be more organized and easier to maintain. This modular approach can lead to clearer, more maintainable code.

Optimized Performance: Different paradigms offer various strengths, such as functional programming's efficient data handling and object-oriented programming's structured design. Integrating these can optimize performance and resource utilization.

Key Steps in Building a Multi-Paradigm Application

Define Application Requirements: Identify the core functionalities and requirements of the application. Determine which paradigms are best suited for different aspects of the application based on these requirements.

Design the Architecture: Plan the architecture to incorporate multiple paradigms effectively. Define how different components will interact and how each paradigm will be utilized within the overall system.

Implement Paradigm-Specific Components:

Object-Oriented Components: Design classes and objects to manage state, represent entities, and encapsulate behaviors.

Functional Components: Use pure functions, higher-order functions, and immutable data to handle data transformations and operations.

Procedural Components: Organize sequences of tasks into functions and procedures to manage workflows and control flow.

Ensure Integration: Integrate components developed using different paradigms to ensure seamless operation. Pay attention to how data flows between functional, object-oriented, and procedural parts of the application.

Testing and Optimization: Test the application thoroughly to ensure that all components work together correctly and that the application meets performance and functionality requirements. Optimize the code as needed to improve efficiency and maintainability.

Documentation and Maintenance: Document the use of different paradigms and their roles in the application. Maintain the code by addressing any issues that arise and by incorporating new features or paradigms as necessary.

PLANNING AND DESIGNING YOUR APPLICATION

Planning and designing your application is a critical phase that sets the foundation for successful software development. This stage involves defining the application's goals, identifying requirements, and creating a blueprint that guides the development process. Effective planning and design ensure that the application meets user needs, adheres to best practices, and is built on a solid architectural framework.

Why Planning and Designing is Crucial
Clarifies Objectives: A well-defined plan helps clarify the application's purpose, features, and target audience. This clarity ensures that all stakeholders have a shared understanding of what the application aims to achieve.

Prevents Scope Creep: By establishing clear requirements and design specifications, planning helps manage expectations and prevents scope creep—where additional features or changes lead to project delays and increased costs.

Guides Development: A detailed design provides a roadmap for developers, outlining the architecture, component interactions, and technology stack. This guidance helps streamline development and reduce the risk of costly mistakes.

Facilitates Communication: Effective planning and design documents facilitate communication among team members, stakeholders, and clients. They serve as a reference point throughout the development process, ensuring everyone is aligned with the project's goals and progress.

Key Steps in Planning and Designing Your Application

Define Objectives and Requirements:

Identify Goals: Determine what the application is intended to accomplish and the problems it aims to solve.
Gather Requirements: Collect and document functional and non-functional requirements from stakeholders and end-users.

Develop a System Architecture:

Design the Architecture: Create a high-level architecture that outlines the overall structure of the application, including major components and their interactions.

Choose Technologies: Select appropriate technologies, frameworks, and tools that align with the application's requirements and design.

Create Detailed Design Specifications:

Design Components: Define the design of individual components, including data models, user interfaces, and business logic.

Establish Interfaces: Plan how components will interact with each other and with external systems.

Plan for Scalability and Performance:

Design for Scalability: Ensure that the application architecture can handle growth in users, data, and functionality.

Optimize Performance: Identify potential performance bottlenecks and plan for optimization strategies.

Prepare for Testing and Maintenance:

Define Testing Strategies: Develop a plan for testing the application to ensure it meets quality standards and performs as expected.

Plan for Maintenance: Outline procedures for maintaining and updating the application post-launch.

Conclusion

Planning and designing your application is essential for creating a successful software solution. By clearly defining objectives, developing a solid architecture, and detailing design specifications, you establish a strong foundation for the development process. This thorough preparation helps ensure that the application meets user needs, performs well, and is built to last.

Requirements Gathering and System Design

Requirements Gathering and System Design are pivotal steps in the software development process that lay the groundwork for a successful application. These stages involve identifying what the application needs to achieve and how it will be structured to meet those needs. Here's a closer look at each component:

1. Requirements Gathering

Requirements gathering is the process of collecting and documenting what stakeholders need from the application. This step ensures that the development team understands the problem to be solved and the features to be included.

Key Activities:

Stakeholder Interviews: Engage with stakeholders such as clients, end-users, and business analysts to gather insights into their needs, preferences, and expectations. Conduct interviews to discuss goals, pain points, and desired outcomes.

Surveys and Questionnaires: Use surveys and questionnaires to collect quantitative and qualitative data from a larger audience. This approach helps in understanding broader user needs and preferences.

Use Case Analysis: Develop use cases that describe how users will interact with the application. Use cases help in defining functional requirements by illustrating various scenarios and user interactions.

Requirement Workshops: Organize workshops with stakeholders to discuss and prioritize requirements collaboratively. Workshops facilitate brainstorming and consensus-building.

Document Analysis: Review existing documentation, such as business process documents, competitor analyses, and system logs, to identify requirements and constraints.

Outcome:

Requirements Specification Document: A detailed document that outlines functional and non-functional requirements, user needs, and constraints. This document serves as a reference throughout the development process to ensure alignment with stakeholder expectations.

2. System Design

System design involves creating a blueprint for how the application will be structured and how its components will interact. This phase translates requirements into a technical framework and design specifications.

Key Activities:

Architectural Design: Develop the overall architecture of the application, including high-level components, their interactions, and the data flow. Decide on the software architecture style (e.g., microservices, monolithic, layered).

Component Design: Define the design of individual components or modules, including their responsibilities, interfaces, and interactions. Determine how components will be organized and communicate with each other.

Data Modeling: Create data models that represent the structure of the application's data. Design databases, data schemas, and relationships between data entities.

User Interface (UI) Design: Design the application's user interfaces, focusing on usability and user experience. Develop wireframes, prototypes, and design specifications for UI elements.

System Integration Planning: Plan how different components and external systems will be integrated. Define integration points, data exchange formats, and protocols.

Scalability and Performance Planning: Design the system to handle expected loads and performance requirements. Consider scalability options, such as load balancing and distributed systems.

Outcome:

System Design Document: A comprehensive document that outlines the system architecture, component designs, data models, and integration plans. This document guides developers and ensures that the application is built according to the specified design.

Conclusion

Requirements Gathering and System Design are crucial for building an effective and reliable application. By thoroughly gathering requirements and meticulously designing the system, developers can ensure that the application meets stakeholder needs, performs well, and is scalable and maintainable. This careful preparation helps in avoiding costly changes later in the development process and sets the stage for a successful software project.

Choosing the Right Paradigms for Each Component

Choosing the right programming paradigms for different components of an application is essential for optimizing performance, maintainability, and scalability. Each paradigm—object-oriented, functional, and procedural—offers distinct advantages that can be leveraged based on the specific needs of each component. Here's a guide to help you select the most appropriate paradigms for various parts of your application:

1. Object-Oriented Programming (OOP)

When to Use:

Complex Data Models: Use OOP for components that involve complex data structures and relationships, such as user profiles, product catalogs, or financial transactions. OOP's encapsulation and inheritance features help manage complexity by organizing data and behavior into manageable objects.

State Management: OOP is ideal for managing stateful components where objects need to maintain and update their internal state. For example, in a graphical user interface (GUI) application, OOP can be used to handle different UI elements and their interactions.

Code Reusability and Extensibility: Utilize OOP when you need to create reusable components and extend functionalities. Inheritance and polymorphism allow for building upon existing classes and creating flexible, modular systems.

Examples:

E-commerce Platforms: Use OOP to model products, customers, orders, and transactions as distinct classes with properties and methods.
Game Development: Employ OOP to represent game entities like players, enemies, and items, encapsulating their attributes and behaviors.

2. Functional Programming (FP)

When to Use:

Data Transformation and Analysis: FP is well-suited for components that involve processing and transforming data.

Its emphasis on pure functions and immutability makes it ideal for handling complex data transformations and avoiding side effects.

Concurrency and Parallelism: Use FP to manage concurrent and parallel processing. Functional programming techniques, such as map-reduce and higher-order functions, can simplify working with large datasets and parallel computations.

Stateless Operations: FP is advantageous for components that perform stateless operations where data is passed and processed without modifying external state. This can improve reliability and testability.

Examples:

Data Processing Pipelines: Implement FP to build data processing pipelines that transform and analyze large volumes of data efficiently.
Financial Calculations: Use FP for calculating financial metrics or performing statistical analysis where immutability and pure functions ensure accuracy and ease of testing.

3. Procedural Programming

When to Use:

Simple Task Management: Use procedural programming for components that involve straightforward, linear tasks and control flow. Procedural programming excels in organizing and executing sequences of operations.

Legacy Code Integration: If working with existing codebases or integrating with legacy systems, procedural programming may be appropriate for maintaining compatibility and consistency.

Performance-Critical Sections: For performance-critical components where low-level control over operations and memory is needed, procedural programming provides a direct approach to optimizing performance.

Examples:

Utility Scripts: Implement procedural programming for utility scripts that perform specific tasks, such as file manipulation or data validation.
Algorithm Implementation: Use procedural code to implement core algorithms or computational routines that require precise control over execution flow.

4. Hybrid Approaches
When to Use:

Complex Applications: For complex applications, a hybrid approach that combines paradigms can be highly effective. Leverage OOP for managing state and structure, FP for data manipulation and transformations, and procedural programming for straightforward tasks and performance optimization.

Modular Development: Combine paradigms to create modular components where each module utilizes the most suitable paradigm for its specific functionality. This can lead to a more maintainable and adaptable codebase.

Examples:

Web Applications: Employ OOP for managing user sessions and state, FP for handling data transformations and API interactions, and procedural programming for backend logic and routing.
Enterprise Systems: Use OOP for business logic and data models, FP for data processing and analytics, and procedural code for task automation and system integration.

Conclusion

Choosing the right paradigms for each component of your application involves understanding the strengths of each paradigm and aligning them with the specific requirements of each component. By strategically applying object-oriented, functional, and procedural programming, you can optimize your application's design, improve code maintainability, and enhance overall performance. A thoughtful approach to paradigm selection ensures that each part of the application is built using the most appropriate and effective techniques.

IMPLEMENTING AND TESTING YOUR APPLICATION

Implementing and Testing Your Application are critical phases in the software development lifecycle where design concepts are transformed into functional software and validated for quality and performance. These stages ensure that the application not only meets the specified requirements but also performs reliably and efficiently in real-world scenarios.

1. Implementation

Implementation is the process of translating the system design and requirements into actual code. This stage involves coding, integrating components, and creating the application's functionality according to the predefined specifications.

Key Activities:

Coding: Write code based on the design specifications, following best practices and coding standards. Focus on implementing features, business logic, and user interfaces as described in the design documents.

Integration: Integrate various components and modules to form a cohesive application. Ensure that different parts of the system work together seamlessly and that data flows correctly between components.

Version Control: Use version control systems to manage code changes and collaborate with team members. Commit changes regularly and use branching strategies to handle different development tasks.

Documentation: Document the implementation process, including code comments, API documentation, and user guides. Proper documentation helps in understanding and maintaining the codebase.

2. Testing

Testing is the process of evaluating the application to ensure it meets quality standards and performs as expected. This phase involves identifying and fixing defects, verifying functionality, and ensuring that the application is reliable and user-friendly.

Key Activities:

Unit Testing: Test individual components or functions in isolation to verify their correctness. Unit tests focus on specific parts of the codebase and ensure that each component performs its intended function.

Integration Testing: Test the interaction between integrated components to ensure that they work together as expected. Integration tests help identify issues related to data flow and component interactions.

System Testing: Test the complete application as a whole to verify that it meets all requirements and functions correctly in the intended environment. System testing includes functional, performance, and security testing.

User Acceptance Testing (UAT): Conduct testing with end-users to validate that the application meets their needs and expectations. UAT helps ensure that the application is user-friendly and satisfies real-world use cases.

Performance Testing: Assess the application's performance under various conditions, such as load, stress, and scalability testing. Performance tests help identify bottlenecks and optimize the application's responsiveness and efficiency.

Regression Testing: Re-test the application after making changes or adding new features to ensure that existing functionality remains unaffected. Regression testing helps maintain software quality throughout the development cycle.

Conclusion

Implementing and Testing Your Application are essential steps in delivering a high-quality software product. Implementation translates design into functional code, while testing ensures that the application meets requirements, performs well, and is free of defects. By carefully executing these phases, you can create a reliable, effective, and user-friendly application that meets both technical and business objectives.

Writing and Testing Code in Different Paradigms

Writing and Testing Code in Different Paradigms involves applying the principles of various programming paradigms—object-oriented, functional, and procedural—to develop and validate software components. Each paradigm has its own methodologies for coding and testing, and understanding these differences helps in leveraging their strengths effectively.

1. Writing Code in Different Paradigms

Object-Oriented Programming (OOP):

Coding Practices:

Class Design: Define classes that encapsulate data and behavior. Use inheritance to create hierarchical relationships and polymorphism to handle different implementations of the same interface.

Encapsulation: Manage internal states using private attributes and provide public methods for interaction.

Abstraction: Create abstract classes and interfaces to define common behaviors and enforce contracts.

Example: In a shopping cart application, you might have classes like Product, Cart, and Customer, each with specific methods and attributes.

Functional Programming (FP):

Coding Practices:

Pure Functions: Write functions that have no side effects and return the same output for the same input.

Immutable Data: Use immutable data structures to ensure that data cannot be modified after creation.

Higher-Order Functions: Employ functions that take other functions as arguments or return them as results, enabling powerful data transformations.

Example: In a data processing pipeline, you might use functions like map, filter, and reduce to process lists of data in a declarative manner.

Procedural Programming:

Coding Practices:

Function-Based Organization: Organize code into functions or procedures that perform specific tasks or operations.

Sequential Execution: Structure code to execute in a linear sequence, focusing on clear, step-by-step logic.

Modularity: Divide the program into modules or functions that handle different aspects of the task.

Example: In a script that processes user input, you might write procedures for reading data, validating input, and generating output sequentially.

2. Testing Code in Different Paradigms
Object-Oriented Programming (OOP):

Unit Testing: Test individual classes and their methods. Use mocking frameworks to simulate interactions between objects and isolate tests.

Integration Testing: Verify interactions between classes and ensure that class hierarchies and relationships work as expected.

Behavioral Testing: Test for correct implementation of design patterns and class behaviors, ensuring that polymorphic methods and inherited features function correctly.

Example: Use tools like JUnit for Java or unittest for Python to write tests for classes and methods in your object-oriented application.

Functional Programming (FP):

Unit Testing: Test individual pure functions by providing input and verifying output. Since functions are stateless, these tests focus on ensuring correctness of logic.

Property-Based Testing: Test properties of functions, such as commutativity or associativity, to ensure they hold under a variety of input conditions.

Integration Testing: Validate that composed functions and data pipelines produce the expected results when integrated.

Example: Use tools like Hypothesis for Python or QuickCheck for Haskell to test properties of functional code.

Procedural Programming:

Unit Testing: Test individual functions to ensure they perform their intended tasks correctly. Focus on edge cases and ensure that each function handles various inputs properly.

Integration Testing: Test sequences of functions or procedures to verify that they work together to achieve the desired outcome.

Performance Testing: Evaluate the efficiency of procedural code, especially in performance-critical applications, to ensure that it meets required benchmarks.

Example: Use tools like pytest for Python or CUnit for C to write and run tests for procedural code.

Conclusion

Writing and Testing Code in Different Paradigms involves adapting coding and testing practices to fit the principles of object-oriented, functional, and procedural programming. By understanding the unique characteristics of each paradigm, developers can write more effective code and apply appropriate testing strategies to ensure that each component of the application functions correctly and efficiently. This approach helps in leveraging the strengths of different paradigms to build robust and high-quality software.

Debugging and Optimizing for Performance

Debugging and Optimizing for Performance are crucial aspects of software development aimed at ensuring that applications run correctly and efficiently. Debugging involves identifying and fixing errors or issues in the code, while optimization focuses on improving the performance of the application. Here's a comprehensive overview of these processes:

1. Debugging

Debugging is the process of locating and resolving bugs or defects in the software to ensure it behaves as expected. Effective debugging helps in maintaining code quality and ensuring that applications meet their functional requirements.

Key Activities:

Reproducing the Issue: Begin by reproducing the bug or issue consistently. Understanding the conditions under which the problem occurs is essential for effective debugging.

Using Debugging Tools: Utilize debugging tools and environments, such as integrated debuggers in IDEs (e.g., PyCharm, Visual Studio Code), to step through the code, set breakpoints, and inspect variables. Tools like gdb for

C/C++ or pdb for Python can help in analyzing and controlling code execution.

Analyzing Logs: Review application logs to trace the sequence of events leading up to the issue. Logs provide valuable insights into the application's state and can help identify anomalies or errors.

Isolating the Problem: Break down the code into smaller sections or components to isolate the problematic area. This approach helps in narrowing down the source of the bug and simplifies the troubleshooting process.

Reviewing Code Changes: Check recent changes or commits to identify any modifications that might have introduced the issue. Version control systems like Git can facilitate this by comparing code versions.

Testing Hypotheses: Formulate hypotheses about potential causes of the issue and test them systematically. This methodical approach helps in identifying the root cause of the problem.

Peer Review: Seek assistance from colleagues or team members to review the code and provide additional perspectives. Collaborative debugging can uncover issues that might be overlooked by an individual.

Best Practices:

Write Unit Tests: Implement unit tests to catch bugs early and ensure code correctness. Automated tests help in identifying issues introduced by code changes.

Maintain Clear Code: Write clean, readable code with meaningful comments to facilitate easier debugging. Clear code helps in understanding the logic and locating errors more efficiently.

2. Optimizing for Performance

Optimizing for Performance involves improving the efficiency of an application to enhance its speed, responsiveness, and overall performance. Optimization is crucial for ensuring that the application can handle high loads and perform well under various conditions.

Key Activities:

Profiling: Use profiling tools to measure the performance of different parts of the application. Profiling helps identify bottlenecks, such as slow functions or high memory usage. Tools like cProfile for Python or VisualVM for Java can assist in performance analysis.

Analyzing Bottlenecks: Examine the results of profiling to locate performance bottlenecks. Focus on sections of code that consume the most resources or take the longest time to execute.

Optimizing Algorithms: Improve the efficiency of algorithms used in the application. Optimize data structures and algorithms to reduce time complexity and memory usage.

Efficient Resource Management: Manage system resources effectively, including memory, CPU, and I/O operations. Use techniques like caching, lazy loading, and efficient data access to enhance performance.

Code Refactoring: Refactor code to eliminate inefficiencies and improve readability. Simplify complex logic and remove redundant code to enhance performance and maintainability.

Parallelism and Concurrency: Utilize parallel processing and concurrency to improve performance for tasks that can be executed simultaneously. Techniques like multi-threading, asynchronous programming, and parallel computing can boost application performance.

Database Optimization: Optimize database queries and indexes to improve data retrieval and manipulation performance. Ensure that database operations are efficient and minimize the impact on overall application performance.

Best Practices:

Measure Before and After: Always measure performance before and after making optimizations to ensure that changes have the desired effect. This helps in quantifying improvements and avoiding unnecessary changes.

Prioritize Optimizations: Focus on optimizing the most critical parts of the application that have the greatest impact on performance. Address high-impact areas first before tackling minor issues.

Avoid Premature Optimization: Avoid optimizing code prematurely before identifying actual performance bottlenecks. Optimize based on data and profiling results rather than assumptions.

Conclusion

Debugging and Optimizing for Performance are essential activities that ensure software applications are reliable, efficient, and performant. Debugging helps in identifying and resolving issues that affect functionality, while optimization focuses on improving application speed and resource usage. By employing effective debugging techniques and performance optimization strategies, developers can deliver high-quality software that meets user expectations and performs well under various conditions.

PART VI: PYTHON TOOLS AND BEST PRACTICES

CHAPTER 11.
Essential Tools for Python Development

Essential Tools for Python Development encompass a range of software and utilities that enhance productivity, streamline development processes, and ensure code quality. These tools cater to various aspects of the development lifecycle, from coding and debugging to testing and deployment. Utilizing the right tools can significantly improve efficiency and effectiveness in Python programming.

Overview

Python development involves several stages, including writing, testing, debugging, and deploying code. Each stage benefits from specialized tools designed to simplify and optimize tasks. By leveraging these tools, developers can manage their projects more effectively, maintain code quality, and accelerate the development process.

Key Categories of Tools:

Integrated Development Environments (IDEs): IDEs provide a comprehensive environment for writing, editing, and debugging code. Popular Python IDEs like PyCharm, Visual Studio Code, and Spyder offer features such as code completion, syntax highlighting, and integrated debugging.

Code Editors: Lightweight editors such as Sublime Text and Atom offer flexibility and speed for writing code. They often come with customizable features and support for various plugins to enhance functionality.

Version Control Systems: Tools like Git and platforms like GitHub or GitLab help manage code versions, collaborate with others, and track changes. Version control is essential for maintaining project history and facilitating team collaboration.

Package Managers: Tools such as pip and conda manage Python packages and dependencies, allowing developers to install, update, and remove libraries efficiently. These tools ensure that projects have the necessary packages for their development and runtime needs.

Testing Frameworks: Testing frameworks like pytest, unittest, and nose provide mechanisms for writing and running tests to ensure code reliability. They support various testing methodologies, including unit testing, integration testing, and functional testing.

Debugging Tools: Debugging tools such as pdb (Python Debugger) and integrated debugging features in IDEs help identify and fix code issues. They provide functionalities like breakpoints, step execution, and variable inspection.

Profiling and Performance Tools: Profiling tools like cProfile and line_profiler help analyze code performance, identify bottlenecks, and optimize efficiency. These tools provide insights into execution time and resource usage.

Build and Deployment Tools: Tools such as setuptools, wheel, and Docker assist in packaging and deploying Python applications. They streamline the process of creating distributable packages and managing application environments.

Conclusion

Essential Tools for Python Development are vital for enhancing productivity, maintaining code quality, and managing the development lifecycle. By selecting and effectively using these tools, developers can improve their workflow, ensure robust and reliable code, and successfully deliver Python applications.

INTEGRATED DEVELOPMENT ENVIRONMENTS (IDEs)

Integrated Development Environments (IDEs) are comprehensive software applications that provide a suite of tools and features to facilitate coding, debugging, and managing software projects. IDEs are designed to enhance developer productivity by integrating various development functions into a single, unified interface. This integration helps streamline the development process, from writing and editing code to debugging and deploying applications.

Overview

IDEs are essential for modern software development, offering a range of functionalities that simplify complex tasks and improve efficiency. They typically include code editors with advanced features, integrated debugging tools, version control support, and project management capabilities. By providing a cohesive environment for coding and managing projects, IDEs enable developers to work more effectively and focus on creating high-quality software.

Key Features of IDEs:

Code Editing: IDEs offer powerful code editors with features such as syntax highlighting, code completion, and error detection. These features help in writing code more efficiently and with fewer errors.

Debugging: Integrated debugging tools allow developers to set breakpoints, step through code, and inspect variables in real time. This capability is crucial for identifying and fixing issues during development.

Version Control Integration: Many IDEs support version control systems like Git, enabling developers to manage code changes, track revisions, and collaborate with team members directly from the IDE.

Project Management: IDEs often include project management tools that help organize files, manage dependencies, and navigate project structures. This organization simplifies the management of large and complex projects.

Build and Run Configurations: IDEs provide facilities for configuring build and run settings, making it easier to compile, run, and test applications. This feature ensures that projects are built and executed consistently.

Extensions and Plugins: Most IDEs support extensions and plugins that add functionality or integrate with other tools and services. This flexibility allows developers to customize their development environment to meet specific needs.

Conclusion

Integrated Development Environments (IDEs) play a critical role in modern software development by providing a comprehensive suite of tools for coding, debugging, and project management. By integrating these functions into a unified interface, IDEs enhance productivity, streamline workflows, and support the development of high-quality software.

Choosing the Right IDE for Your Workflow

Selecting the right Integrated Development Environment (IDE) for your workflow is crucial for maximizing productivity, maintaining code quality, and streamlining the development process. The ideal IDE should align with your project requirements, personal preferences, and the programming languages you use. With numerous IDEs available, each offering unique features and strengths, it's important to consider several factors when making your choice.

Key Factors to Consider:

Programming Language Support:

Ensure that the IDE you choose supports the primary programming language(s) you work with. Some IDEs are tailored for specific languages (e.g., PyCharm for Python, IntelliJ IDEA for Java), while others offer broader support for multiple languages (e.g., Visual Studio Code, Eclipse).

Feature Set:

Consider the features that are most important to your workflow. Essential features might include code completion, syntax highlighting, integrated debugging, and version control integration. Advanced features like refactoring tools, code analysis, and testing frameworks can also enhance your development process.

Ease of Use and Learning Curve:

The usability of an IDE is critical, especially if you're new to the environment. Some IDEs, like Visual Studio Code, are known for their intuitive interfaces and ease of use, while others may have a steeper learning curve but offer more powerful features.

Performance and Resource Usage:

IDEs can vary significantly in terms of performance and resource consumption. Lightweight editors like Sublime Text and Atom are faster and consume fewer resources, making them suitable for smaller projects or less powerful machines. In contrast, feature-rich IDEs like PyCharm or IntelliJ IDEA might require more system resources but offer a more comprehensive development experience.

Customization and Extensibility:

Consider how customizable the IDE is and whether it supports extensions or plugins. IDEs like Visual Studio Code and JetBrains IDEs offer extensive marketplaces for extensions, allowing you to tailor the environment to your specific needs.

Integration with Tools and Workflows:

Your IDE should integrate well with other tools and services you use, such as version control systems (e.g., Git), build tools, testing frameworks, and deployment pipelines. Seamless integration can significantly streamline your workflow.

Community and Support:

A strong community and good support resources are valuable when choosing an IDE. Popular IDEs often have extensive documentation, tutorials, and active communities that can help you troubleshoot issues or learn new features. Cost:

While many IDEs are free and open-source (e.g., Visual Studio Code, Eclipse), others might require a license or subscription (e.g., JetBrains products like PyCharm or IntelliJ IDEA). Consider your budget and whether the paid features justify the cost for your particular needs.

Popular IDEs to Consider:

Visual Studio Code: A lightweight, highly customizable editor with a vast library of extensions, suitable for a wide range of languages and workflows.

PyCharm: A powerful, feature-rich IDE specifically designed for Python development, offering advanced debugging, testing, and code analysis tools.

IntelliJ IDEA: A robust IDE with excellent support for Java and other JVM languages, as well as comprehensive features for web and enterprise development.

Eclipse: A long-standing, versatile IDE that supports multiple programming languages and is widely used for Java development.

Sublime Text: A fast and lightweight code editor with a simple interface, known for its speed and ease of use, especially for smaller projects.

Conclusion

Choosing the Right IDE for Your Workflow involves carefully evaluating your development needs, the languages you use, and the features that are most important to you. The right IDE can greatly enhance your productivity and the quality of your work, so it's worth investing time to explore different options and select the one that best aligns with your workflow. Whether you prioritize performance, customization, or a comprehensive feature set, there's an IDE out there that can meet your needs and help you develop efficiently and effectively.

Maximizing Productivity with IDE Features

Integrated Development Environments (IDEs) are powerful tools designed to streamline the software development process, enabling developers to write, test, debug, and deploy code more efficiently. To fully leverage the potential of an IDE, it's important to understand and utilize the various features it offers. By doing so, you can significantly boost your productivity, reduce errors, and accelerate the development cycle.

Key IDE Features to Boost Productivity:

Code Completion and IntelliSense:

Code completion, often referred to as IntelliSense, helps you write code faster and with fewer errors by suggesting completions for partially typed words, method names, and variable names. This feature reduces the need for constant referencing of documentation and ensures consistency in code.

Syntax Highlighting and Error Detection:

Syntax highlighting visually differentiates elements of your code (e.g., keywords, variables, strings) using different colors, making it easier to read and understand. Additionally, many IDEs provide real-time error detection, flagging syntax errors or potential issues as you type, allowing you to address problems immediately.

Refactoring Tools:

Refactoring tools simplify the process of restructuring existing code without changing its external behavior. Common refactoring actions include renaming variables, extracting methods, and reorganizing code structures. These tools help maintain clean, readable, and maintainable code, especially as projects grow in size and complexity.

Integrated Debugging:

Integrated debugging tools allow you to set breakpoints, step through code, and inspect variables in real time. By using these tools, you can quickly identify and resolve bugs, leading to more reliable and robust code. Debuggers also provide insight into how code is executed, which is invaluable for optimizing performance.

Version Control Integration:

Built-in version control features, often integrated with Git, allow you to manage code changes, create branches, and merge updates without leaving your IDE. This integration simplifies collaboration with team members, helps track changes over time, and facilitates seamless rollbacks to previous versions if necessary.

Live Templates and Snippets:

IDEs often include live templates and code snippets—predefined pieces of code that can be quickly inserted into your project. These are especially useful for repetitive tasks or complex code patterns, saving you time and ensuring consistency across your codebase.

Unit Testing Integration:

Many IDEs support integration with testing frameworks like pytest, JUnit, or NUnit, allowing you to write, run, and debug tests directly within the IDE. Running tests frequently helps catch bugs early in the development process and ensures that your code remains reliable as it evolves.

Project and File Management:

IDEs provide tools for managing large projects with many files and dependencies. Features such as project explorers, file search, and dependency management help you navigate and organize your codebase efficiently, reducing the time spent on routine file management tasks.

Build Automation:

Build automation tools integrated into IDEs streamline the process of compiling code, packaging applications, and running automated tests. By automating these tasks, you can reduce manual errors and save time, especially when working on large or complex projects.

Extensions and Plugins:

Most modern IDEs support a wide range of extensions and plugins that add additional functionality or integrate with other tools and services. By customizing your IDE with the right extensions, you can tailor it to your specific workflow, further enhancing productivity.

Best Practices for Maximizing IDE Productivity:

Customize Your IDE: Adjust settings, shortcuts, and themes to match your preferences and workflow. This personalization can reduce friction and make the development process more intuitive.

Learn Keyboard Shortcuts: Mastering keyboard shortcuts for common tasks (e.g., navigation, refactoring, code formatting) can significantly speed up your workflow and reduce reliance on the mouse.

Use Extensions Wisely: Choose extensions that genuinely enhance your workflow and avoid overloading your IDE with unnecessary plugins that could slow it down or complicate its use.

Regularly Update Your IDE: Keep your IDE and its plugins up-to-date to benefit from the latest features, bug fixes, and performance improvements.

Conclusion

Maximizing Productivity with IDE Features involves fully understanding and utilizing the powerful tools and functionalities that modern IDEs offer. By taking advantage of features like code completion, integrated debugging, version control integration, and refactoring tools, you can streamline your development process, reduce errors, and enhance the quality of your code. Tailoring your IDE environment to fit your workflow and regularly exploring new features can lead to significant gains in productivity and efficiency.

VERSION CONTROL AND COLLABORATION

In today's software development landscape, version control systems (VCS) and collaboration tools are essential for managing codebases, tracking changes, and facilitating teamwork. Whether you're working on a solo project or as part of a large development team, using a VCS like Git allows you to maintain a history of your code, experiment with new features without disrupting the main codebase, and easily collaborate with others.

Version control not only helps in preserving different versions of your project but also makes it easier to manage contributions from multiple developers, ensuring that everyone is working on the most up-to-date code. When integrated with collaboration platforms like GitHub, GitLab, or Bitbucket, version control systems provide a centralized location for code reviews, issue tracking, and continuous integration, enhancing the overall development workflow.

In this section, we'll explore the fundamentals of version control, the importance of branching and merging strategies, and how to effectively use these tools to collaborate on code, resolve conflicts, and maintain a clean, organized codebase. By mastering these concepts, you'll be better equipped to handle complex projects, streamline collaboration, and contribute effectively to open-source or enterprise-level projects.

Using Git for Source Control

Git is the most widely used version control system (VCS) in the software development world today, known for its flexibility, speed, and powerful features. It enables developers to track changes in their code, collaborate with others seamlessly, and maintain a clear history of project evolution. Whether you are working on a solo project or as part of a team, Git is an essential tool for managing source code effectively.

Key Concepts of Git:

Repositories:

A Git repository (repo) is where all the project files and their history are stored. Repositories can be local (on your machine) or remote (hosted on a service like GitHub, GitLab, or Bitbucket), allowing you to synchronize your code across different environments and collaborate with others.

Commits:

A commit in Git is a snapshot of your code at a specific point in time. Each commit includes a message describing the changes made, which helps in tracking the progress and reasoning behind changes over time. Commits are the building blocks of a project's history in Git.

Branches:

Branches are separate lines of development that allow you to work on different features or fixes simultaneously without affecting the main codebase. The main branch (often called main or master) usually contains the stable version of the project, while other branches are used for development or experimentation.

Merging:

Merging is the process of integrating changes from one branch into another. This allows you to bring together different lines of development, such as combining new features from a development branch into the main branch. Git's ability to handle merges efficiently is one of its strongest features.

Staging Area:

Before changes are committed, they are first placed in the staging area (or index). This allows you to group related changes together and review them before making a commit. Only the files in the staging area are included in the next commit, giving you fine-grained control over what gets committed.

Remote Repositories:

Remote repositories are hosted versions of your Git repository on platforms like GitHub or GitLab. They serve as the central source of truth for a project, allowing team members to push their changes and pull updates from others. This facilitates collaboration and ensures everyone is working with the latest code.

Pull Requests (PRs):

Pull requests (also known as merge requests in some platforms) are a feature used to propose changes in a project by requesting that someone review and merge your branch into the main branch. PRs are commonly used in collaborative workflows to ensure code quality and discuss changes before they are integrated.

Basic Git Workflow:

Clone a Repository:

To start working on an existing project, you would typically clone a remote repository to your local machine. This creates a local copy of the entire project and its history.
bash
Copy code
git clone https://github.com/user/repository.git

Create a Branch:

Before making changes, create a new branch for your work. This keeps your changes isolated until they are ready to be merged.
bash
Copy code
git checkout -b feature-branch

Stage and Commit Changes:

After making changes, add them to the staging area and commit them with a descriptive message.

bash

Copy code

```
git add .
git commit -m "Add feature X"
```

Push to Remote:

Push your branch to the remote repository to share your work with others.

bash

Copy code

```
git push origin feature-branch
```

Open a Pull Request:

On platforms like GitHub, you can then open a pull request to propose your changes for review.

Merge and Delete Branch:

Once the pull request is approved, merge the changes into the main branch and delete the feature branch if it's no longer needed.

bash

```
Copy code
git checkout main
git merge feature-branch
git branch -d feature-branch
```

Advantages of Using Git:

Distributed Nature: Every developer has a complete local copy of the repository, including the entire history, allowing for offline work and better collaboration.

Efficient Branching and Merging: Git makes it easy to create, manage, and merge branches, enabling smooth parallel development.

Trackable History: Every change is recorded with a commit message, making it easy to track down the source of bugs or understand the evolution of the project.

Collaboration: With remote repositories, multiple developers can work together seamlessly, contributing to the same project from anywhere in the world.

Conclusion

Using Git for source control is a fundamental skill for any developer, providing the tools needed to manage code effectively, collaborate with others, and maintain a clean, organized project history. By mastering Git's key concepts and workflows, you can significantly enhance your productivity and contribute to projects with confidence, knowing that your code is well-managed and easy to track.

Collaborating with Teams on Python Projects

Collaboration is an essential aspect of modern software development, especially in Python projects, where multiple developers often work together to build and maintain complex applications. Successful collaboration requires not just technical skills, but also effective communication, clear workflows, and a well-organized codebase. Leveraging tools like version control systems (such as Git), issue trackers, and continuous integration (CI) services can help teams work together efficiently, ensuring that the project progresses smoothly and that the code remains high quality.

Key Aspects of Team Collaboration:

Version Control with Git:

Using Git is crucial for collaborative development. It allows multiple developers to work on the same project simultaneously without overwriting each other's changes. With Git, you can create branches for new features, track progress, review changes, and merge updates seamlessly. Teams can also use pull requests to review code before it is merged into the main branch, ensuring that all contributions meet the project's quality standards.

.

Establishing a Workflow:

To avoid confusion and conflicts, it's essential to establish a clear workflow. Common workflows include Git Flow, GitHub Flow, and Trunk-Based Development. Each team member should understand when and how to create branches, commit changes, merge branches, and resolve conflicts. Regular communication and adherence to the workflow ensure that everyone is on the same page.

Code Reviews:

Code reviews are a critical part of the collaboration process. They help catch bugs, improve code quality, and ensure that the code adheres to the project's standards. Reviews also provide an opportunity for knowledge sharing, where team members can learn from each other's approaches and solutions. Tools like GitHub, GitLab, and Bitbucket provide built-in features for conducting code reviews.

Issue Tracking and Project Management:

Effective collaboration involves managing tasks, tracking bugs, and prioritizing work. Tools like Jira, Trello, or GitHub Issues allow teams to assign tasks, set deadlines, and monitor progress. These tools help keep the project organized and ensure that everyone knows what they are working on and what the priorities are.

Continuous Integration/Continuous Deployment (CI/CD):

CI/CD pipelines automatically build, test, and deploy code changes whenever a team member pushes updates to the repository. This ensures that any integration issues are caught early, and the project remains in a deployable state. Popular CI/CD tools like Jenkins, Travis CI, and GitHub

Actions help streamline the development process and reduce the chances of bugs reaching production.

Communication:

Effective communication is the backbone of any successful team. Using platforms like Slack, Microsoft Teams, or Discord allows team members to stay in touch, discuss issues in real-time, and collaborate on problem-solving. Regular stand-ups, sprint planning meetings, and retrospectives help keep the team aligned and the project on track.

Documentation:

Comprehensive documentation is crucial for team collaboration. It includes everything from code comments and API documentation to README files and contribution guidelines. Clear documentation ensures that all team members can understand the project's structure, use the code correctly, and contribute effectively.

Shared Development Environments:

In some cases, teams may benefit from using shared development environments or containerized setups (e.g., using Docker) to ensure consistency across different development machines. This approach reduces the likelihood of "it works on my machine" issues and ensures that the entire team is working in the same environment.

Best Practices for Team Collaboration:

Regularly Sync Your Work: Frequently pull the latest changes from the main branch to keep your local environment up to date and avoid conflicts.

Keep Commits Small and Focused: Aim for small, atomic commits that address a single issue or feature. This makes it easier to track changes and identify the source of problems.

Write Clear Commit Messages: Commit messages should be descriptive and provide context about the changes made. This is important for future reference and for team members reviewing your code.

Use Feature Branches: Always develop new features or fixes in separate branches. This keeps the main branch stable and allows for easier rollbacks if needed.

Automate Testing: Implement automated testing to catch issues early. This ensures that new changes do not introduce bugs or break existing functionality.

Respect Code Ownership: While collaboration is key, it's important to respect the ownership of different parts of the codebase. Consult with the original author before making significant changes.

Conclusion

Collaborating on Python projects requires more than just coding skills—it requires a well-structured approach to teamwork. By using Git for version control, establishing clear workflows, conducting thorough code reviews, and maintaining open communication, teams can work together effectively to build robust, high-quality applications. Leveraging tools like issue trackers and CI/CD pipelines further enhances productivity and ensures that projects are delivered on time and meet the desired standards. Ultimately, successful collaboration depends on clear processes, mutual respect, and a shared commitment to the project's goals.

CHAPTER 12

Writing Clean and Maintainable Python Code

Writing clean and maintainable code is essential for any successful software project. In Python, where readability is a core principle of the language, adhering to best practices in code cleanliness is especially important. Clean code is not only easier to read and understand but also simpler to debug, extend, and maintain over time. This becomes increasingly significant in collaborative environments, where multiple developers may need to work on the same codebase.

In this section, we'll explore strategies for writing Python code that is both clean and maintainable. We'll cover essential topics such as following the PEP 8 style guide, organizing code effectively, writing clear and concise comments, and employing meaningful variable and function names. Additionally, we'll discuss the importance of refactoring, testing, and using design patterns where appropriate.

By adopting these practices, you can ensure that your Python code remains robust, efficient, and easy to manage, whether you're working on small scripts or large-scale applications.

FOLLOWING PYTHONIC CONVENTIONS

In Python programming, adhering to "Pythonic" conventions is crucial for writing code that is not only functional but also elegant and idiomatic. The term "Pythonic" refers to the principles and style guidelines that embrace Python's design philosophy, emphasizing readability, simplicity, and the use of Python's unique features. Following these conventions ensures that your code aligns with the expectations of the Python community, making it easier for others to understand and collaborate on.

This section will delve into key Pythonic conventions, including adherence to the PEP 8 style guide, leveraging Python's expressive syntax, and employing best practices for code clarity and consistency. By following these conventions, you'll produce code that is more readable, maintainable, and idiomatic, ultimately leading to better collaboration and easier long-term management of your projects.

Understanding PEP 8 Standards

PEP 8, or Python Enhancement Proposal 8, is the style guide for Python code. It provides a set of conventions and guidelines for writing Python code in a way that maximizes readability and consistency. Adhering to PEP 8 standards is considered a best practice in Python development and helps ensure that code is clean, understandable, and maintainable.

Key PEP 8 Guidelines:

Code Layout:

Indentation: Use 4 spaces per indentation level. Avoid using tabs for indentation.
Line Length: Limit all lines to a maximum of 79 characters. For docstrings and comments, limit lines to 72 characters.

Blank Lines: Use blank lines to separate top-level function and class definitions, as well as within functions to separate logical sections of code.

Imports:

Import Formatting: Imports should usually be on separate lines and grouped into standard library imports, third-party imports, and local application imports. Each group should be separated by a blank line.

Import Order: Follow the order: standard library imports, related third-party imports, and then local application imports.

Naming Conventions:

Variables and Functions: Use lowercase words separated by underscores (e.g., my_variable, my_function).

Classes: Use CapitalizedWords convention (e.g., MyClass).

Constants: Use all uppercase letters with underscores separating words (e.g., MY_CONSTANT).

Documentation:

Docstrings: Use triple quotes for docstrings to document modules, classes, and functions. Include a summary of the object's purpose and a description of its parameters and return values.

Comments: Write comments that are clear and concise. Use comments to explain why something is done, not what is done, as the latter should be evident from the code itself.

Code Practices:

Avoid Redundancy: Write code that is simple and avoids unnecessary complexity. Favor straightforward solutions over complex ones.

Error Handling: Use exceptions for error handling rather than returning error codes or using other methods.

Whitespace:

Avoid Extra Spaces: Do not include extra spaces in expressions and statements. For example, avoid spaces around the = sign when used for keyword arguments or default parameters.

Aligning Code: When aligning code, use vertical alignment for readability, but avoid aligning with inconsistent whitespace.

Benefits of Following PEP 8:

Readability: Consistent formatting makes code easier to read and understand, reducing the cognitive load for developers who maintain or review the code.

Consistency: Following PEP 8 ensures uniformity across different codebases and projects, making it easier for developers to switch between projects or work in teams.

Collaboration: Standardized code practices facilitate better collaboration among team members, as everyone adheres to the same conventions and guidelines.

Conclusion

PEP 8 provides a comprehensive framework for writing clean and consistent Python code. By understanding and applying these standards, developers can produce code that is more readable, maintainable, and aligned with the Python community's best practices. Adhering to PEP 8 not only improves the quality of your code but also enhances collaboration and efficiency in development projects.

Writing Code That's Readable and Consistent

Readable and consistent code is the cornerstone of effective software development. It ensures that code is not only understandable to the original author but also to others who may work on or maintain it in the future. This enhances collaboration, reduces the likelihood of bugs, and simplifies the process of making modifications and updates.

Principles of Readable and Consistent Code:
Clarity Over Cleverness:

Prioritize clarity over clever solutions. Code should be straightforward and easy to understand rather than using complex or obscure techniques that might be difficult for others to decipher. Write code that communicates its intent clearly and avoids unnecessary complexity.

Descriptive Naming Conventions:

Use meaningful and descriptive names for variables, functions, classes, and other identifiers. Names should convey the purpose or role of the item in question. For instance, use calculate_average() instead of calc_avg() to make the function's purpose clear.

Consistent Formatting:

Apply consistent formatting throughout your codebase. Follow established style guides, such as PEP 8 for Python, to maintain uniformity in indentation, line length, and spacing. Consistent formatting helps to prevent confusion and makes code easier to navigate.

Commenting and Documentation:

Provide clear and useful comments that explain the rationale behind complex or non-obvious code segments. Use docstrings to document modules, classes, and functions, describing their purpose, parameters, and return values. Avoid redundant comments that restate the obvious and focus on why something is done rather than what is done.

Code Organization:

Organize code logically by grouping related functions, classes, and modules together. Follow a consistent structure for files and directories to make it easier to locate and manage different parts of the codebase. This organization helps maintain a clean and manageable codebase.

Avoiding Hard-Coded Values:

Replace hard-coded values with named constants or configuration parameters. This practice makes your code more flexible and easier to maintain, as changes to these values need to be made in only one place.

Modularity and Reusability:

Write modular code by breaking down large functions or classes into smaller, reusable components. Each module, function, or class should have a single responsibility and be as self-contained as possible. This promotes code reuse and simplifies testing and maintenance.

Consistent Error Handling:

Use consistent error-handling practices throughout your code. Handle exceptions appropriately and provide meaningful error messages that can help diagnose problems. Avoid using generic error handling that can obscure the source of issues.

Refactoring:

Regularly refactor code to improve its readability and maintainability. Refactoring involves restructuring existing code without changing its external behavior to make it cleaner and more efficient. This helps to manage technical debt and keeps the codebase in good shape.

Code Reviews:

Participate in and conduct regular code reviews. Code reviews help identify potential issues, enforce coding standards, and share knowledge among team members. Constructive feedback from peers can greatly enhance code quality and consistency.

Conclusion

Writing code that's readable and consistent is vital for effective software development. By adhering to clear naming conventions, consistent formatting, and best practices for documentation and organization, developers can create code that is easier to understand, maintain, and extend. Prioritizing readability and consistency not only improves individual code quality but also enhances collaboration and overall project success.

TESTING AND DEBUGGING TECHNIQUES

Testing and debugging are essential practices in software development that ensure the reliability, functionality, and quality of code. While testing helps identify and confirm that code behaves as expected, debugging is the process of diagnosing and fixing issues that arise during development or after deployment. Mastering these techniques is crucial for delivering robust and error-free software.

This section will introduce various testing and debugging techniques, including unit testing, integration testing, and automated testing frameworks. It will also cover common debugging strategies, tools, and practices for efficiently diagnosing and resolving issues. By employing these techniques, developers can enhance code quality, reduce bugs, and ensure that their software performs reliably under different conditions.

Unit Testing with PyTest

Unit testing is a fundamental practice in software development that involves testing individual units or components of a program to ensure they function correctly. In Python, one of the most popular tools for unit testing is PyTest, a powerful and flexible testing framework. PyTest is widely used due to its simplicity, ease of use, and ability to handle complex testing scenarios with minimal boilerplate code.

Why Use PyTest?

Simplicity: PyTest allows you to write test cases in a straightforward and concise manner. There's no need for excessive boilerplate code, making it easy to start writing tests right away.

Automatic Test Discovery: PyTest automatically discovers and runs tests, reducing the need for manual configuration. It identifies tests by looking for files, classes, and functions that start with test_.

Rich Plugin Ecosystem: PyTest has a wide range of plugins that extend its functionality, from handling fixtures and mocking to integrating with CI/CD pipelines.

Powerful Assertion Introspection: PyTest provides detailed and user-friendly error messages when assertions fail, making it easier to identify the root cause of test failures.

Getting Started with PyTest
Installation:

You can install PyTest using pip:
bash
Copy code
pip install pytest
Once installed, you can run your tests by simply typing pytest in your terminal. PyTest will automatically discover and execute all test functions.

Writing Your First Test:

Tests in PyTest are typically written in functions. A simple test might look like this:
python
Copy code

```python
# test_example.py
def test_addition():
    assert 1 + 1 == 2


def test_subtraction():
    assert 5 - 3 == 2
```
Save the above code in a file named test_example.py. Running pytest in the terminal will discover and execute these tests.

Using Fixtures:

Fixtures in PyTest allow you to set up a known state before tests are run and clean up afterward. They are useful for managing resources like database connections, temporary files, or pre-configured objects.

Example:
python
Copy code
```python
import pytest


@pytest.fixture
def sample_data():
    return {"key": "value"}
```

```python
def test_sample_data(sample_data):
    assert sample_data["key"] == "value"
```

Parametrized Tests:

PyTest allows you to run the same test with different inputs using parameterization. This is useful when you want to test a function with multiple sets of data.
Example:
python
Copy code

```python
@pytest.mark.parametrize("input,expected", [
    (1 + 1, 2),
    (5 - 3, 2),
    (3 * 3, 9)
])
def test_operations(input, expected):
    assert input == expected
```

Running and Reporting:

Running pytest in the terminal will execute all the discovered tests. PyTest provides a summary of the test results, including details of any failures or errors.

You can add flags to the command for more detailed output, such as pytest -v for verbose mode or pytest --maxfail=3 to stop after a few failures.

Best Practices for Unit Testing with PyTest

Test Small, Isolated Units: Focus on testing individual functions or methods, ensuring they work as expected in isolation.

Write Tests Alongside Code: Adopt test-driven development (TDD) practices by writing tests as you develop features. This ensures that code is always covered by tests.

Use Descriptive Test Names: Name your test functions descriptively to indicate what they are testing. This makes it easier to understand test reports.

Keep Tests Independent: Ensure that tests do not depend on each other. Each test should set up its own environment and not rely on the results of another test.

....

Conclusion

PyTest is a versatile and user-friendly framework that makes unit testing in Python efficient and effective. By leveraging its features—such as fixtures, parameterization, and its plugin ecosystem—you can write comprehensive tests that improve the reliability and maintainability of your code. Unit testing with PyTest should be an integral part of your development workflow, ensuring that each component of your application works correctly and integrates seamlessly with the rest.

Effective Debugging Strategies

Debugging is a critical skill in software development, essential for identifying, diagnosing, and fixing issues in your code. Effective debugging strategies not only save time but also help in understanding the root causes of problems, leading to more robust and maintainable software. Here's a guide to some of the most effective debugging strategies you can employ to tackle issues in your Python code.

1. Reproduce the Problem

The first step in debugging is to reliably reproduce the problem. If you can consistently trigger the bug, you have a better chance of understanding what's causing it. This might involve running the code with specific inputs, in a particular environment, or under certain conditions. Reproducing the issue consistently is crucial because it allows you to test potential fixes effectively.

2. Simplify the Problem

Once the problem is reproducible, the next step is to simplify the scenario as much as possible. Strip down the code to its most basic form that still produces the error. This often involves removing unrelated code, using minimal input data, or isolating the faulty function. Simplifying the problem can help you focus on the specific part of the code that is causing the issue.

3. Use Print Statements Wisely

Adding print statements is one of the simplest and most widely used debugging techniques. By printing out variable values and program states at different points in your code, you can trace the flow of execution and identify where things go wrong. However, be mindful not to overwhelm your code with too many print statements; instead, place them strategically to provide the most insight.

4. Leverage Python's Debugger (pdb)

Python's built-in debugger, pdb, is a powerful tool that allows you to set breakpoints, step through your code line by line, inspect variables, and evaluate expressions at runtime. Using pdb, you can interactively explore your code's behavior as it executes, which is especially useful for tracking down elusive bugs.

To start the debugger, simply import pdb and call pdb.set_trace() at the point in your code where you want to start debugging:

python
Copy code

```
import pdb; pdb.set_trace()
```

This will pause the program execution and open an interactive debugging session at the specified point.

5. Utilize Logging

While print statements are useful, logging offers a more flexible and powerful way to track the behavior of your code. Python's logging module allows you to record messages at different severity levels (e.g., DEBUG, INFO, WARNING, ERROR, CRITICAL), and to direct these messages to different outputs (e.g., console, files).

Logging is especially useful in production environments, where you may need to diagnose issues without direct access to the console. You can set different logging levels to control the verbosity of the output and maintain a clear, organized record of your program's execution.

6. Break Down the Code

When debugging a complex piece of code, it can be helpful to break it down into smaller parts and test each part independently. This modular approach allows you to isolate the section where the error occurs, making it easier to identify the problem. By testing smaller units of code, you can pinpoint where the issue arises without getting lost in the complexity of the entire program.

7. Check for Common Pitfalls

Certain types of bugs are common in programming, such as off-by-one errors, uninitialized variables, or issues with mutable data types. Keeping these common pitfalls in mind can help you identify and fix problems more quickly. For instance, if your program is producing an off-by-one error, double-check any loops or indexing operations to ensure they are correctly implemented.

8. Review the Code with Fresh Eyes

Sometimes, stepping away from your code for a while and coming back with fresh eyes can help you spot the problem more quickly. A fresh perspective can help you see errors or oversights that were not apparent before. Additionally, having a colleague review your code can provide valuable insights, as they may notice issues that you missed.

9. Test Edge Cases

Bugs often appear when the code encounters edge cases—situations at the extreme ends of the input spectrum, such as empty inputs, very large numbers, or unexpected data types. Testing edge cases can help you identify weaknesses in your code that only become apparent under unusual conditions. By proactively testing these scenarios, you can ensure your code handles a wider range of inputs robustly.

10. Use Automated Testing

Incorporating automated testing into your development workflow can significantly reduce the occurrence of bugs and make debugging easier. Unit tests, integration tests, and end-to-end tests can catch issues early in the development process, before they make it into production. When a bug does occur, automated tests can help you quickly identify the part of the code that is failing and provide a starting point for debugging.

Conclusion

Effective debugging is a blend of strategy, tools, and intuition. By following these techniques—reproducing the problem, simplifying the scenario, using print statements and logging, employing pdb, breaking down the code, and considering common pitfalls—you can systematically approach and resolve bugs in your Python code. Developing strong debugging skills will not only help you fix problems faster but also lead to writing more resilient and maintainable software in the long run.